Sue Cowley's A–Z

Other titles by Sue Cowley:

Sue Cowley's Teaching Clinic

How to Survive your First Year in Teaching

Guerilla Guide to Teaching

Getting the Buggers to Behave 2

Getting the Buggers to Think

Getting the Buggers to Write 2

Getting your Little Darlings to Behave

Other related titles from Continuum:

Primary Teacher's Handbook – Lyn Overall and Margaret Sangster

Secondary Teacher's Handbook – Lyn Overall and Margaret Sangster

Teacher's Survival Guide Second Edition – Angela Thody, Derek Bowden and Barbara Gray

Sue Cowley's A–Z of Teaching

Sue Cowley

continuum
LONDON • NEW YORK

Continuum International Publishing Group

The Tower Building   15 East 26th Street
11 York Road   New York
London SE1 7NX   NY 10010

© Sue Cowley 2004

British Library Cataloguing-in-Publication Data
A catalogue record for this book is available from the British Library.

ISBN: 08264 7572 8 (paperback)

Typeset by YHT Ltd, London
Printed in Great Britain by Antony Rowe Ltd, Chippenham, Wiltshire

To my mum, Jill, and my aunt, Monica:
two women who dedicated a large part of their lives
to the teaching profession.

And to John Rust-Andrews,
mentor and friend, who laid the
foundations for my teaching career.

Acknowledgements

Many thanks go to all the staff at Continuum, especially Anthony Haynes, Suzanne Ashley, Katie Sayers, and Christina Parkinson. A special thank you must go to my Editor, Alexandra Webster, for all her hard work on my behalf.

Thanks to all those people in my network of support, who make it possible for me to write for a living, especially Tilak and Álvie, the girls at the October club and all my friends and family. A special thank you to my sister Ally who shares the writing gene – at least this one won't need an index!

Introduction

Need to find your way around the teaching profession? Lost in the classroom without a map? My A–Z of teaching will show you exactly where to go and how to get there. This book is irreverent, cheeky, humorous, and downright subversive in parts (a kind of literary equivalent of the Channel 4 *Teachers* programme). It gives an honest and realistic overview of what being a teacher is really all about. I would advise against reading this book if you are easily offended, if you have a rose-tinted view of the teaching profession, or if you work for the DfES. The truth about what teachers and schools are really like may come as a bit of a shock.

In this book my aim has been to combine an honest explanation and analysis of all the different facets of teaching, with some useful tips about how to manage the more taxing parts of the job. Teaching is a profession stuffed full of jargon and euphemisms, so for those of you new to the profession, or for anyone struggling to keep up with the latest terminology, I've tried to demystify some of the more commonly used language. As well as giving definitions and a commentary about each topic, I have also included a small selection of useful website addresses for further reading.

Teaching is a job in which the theory of what should happen very often outweighs the reality of what actually does go on. In this book I don't pull any punches – I talk about the world of education as it really is, not as we might want or hope it to be in an 'ideal world'. You will find some pointed and personal comments here about the more negative aspects of the profession – I do confess to getting wound up by anything that gets between teachers and the vital job they do in working with children. However, you will also find plenty here that is positive and optimistic. There are so many great things about being a teacher and despite all the hard times and difficulties (or sometimes even *because* of them), it really is one of the best jobs in the world.

Sue Cowley
www.suecowley.co.uk

Please note: where I have used names in telling anecdotes from my own experience, these have been changed to protect the identities of the children, staff and schools involved.

Where website addresses have been given, every attempt has been made to ensure that these are up to date and still in existence. However, please accept that the ever-changing nature of the internet means that some links may have been lost between my writing this book and its publication.

ATTITUDE

To act or behave in a way that makes your opinion or feelings clear.

I have to confess that I have a real soft spot for the kids who have what we teachers call an 'attitude'. These children are not necessarily much fun to deal with in the classroom, but they definitely have a certain something about them. These are the kids with a 'spark', the ones who kick back against the authority of schools and of teachers. In the classic words of Pink Floyd, they believe that they 'don't need no education', and they're not afraid to let us know it.

Attitude comes in many different shapes and sizes. From the student who demands to know 'why should I?' when asked to complete a task, to the child who turns into a miniature version of Gordon Ramsey/Johnny Rotten if you dare to hand out a sanction ('you're a f★★★★★★ c★★★ miss/sir!'). Whatever form of attitude you're dealing with, it's all too easy to get wound up by a child who gives you a hard time. Far better to learn not to take it seriously – after all, if you do react, then the child's attitude is obviously having an impact.

Attitude is not something that floats down out of the sky – there's always a reason for it, and it most likely originates in the home environment. It might be that the child's parents have an equally big and aggressive attitude, and what you see in your classroom is a facsimile of behaviour learned at home (if this is the case, tread carefully at parents' evening). It could be the child has picked up an arrogance about the whole process of school and learning – again, typically something learned early on.

Perhaps surprisingly, some of our most gifted students will demonstrate an impressive level of attitude. For these very able children, school can be a place where long days are spent studying things they already understand, or working at a level that they feel is beneath them. Certainly, we teachers can also be to blame for not stretching or challenging these students sufficiently.

The kids with attitude are the ones who stick in your mind: the ones you remember long after you or they have left a school. These are the children who, for some reason that you can't quite pinpoint, seemed somehow 'special'. Perhaps the challenge of developing positive relationships with these children means we value the steps we take together that much more?

I still remember Charlie vividly. He had a cheeky smile, a wicked way with the language of the streets, and an attitude the size of Greater London. A number of teachers had already told me how difficult he (and indeed, that class) was to deal with, and I was more than a little apprehensive in our opening lesson. But to approach a class or a student expecting the worst is simply not fair. No matter how difficult they make life for other teachers, it's only right that we should judge our students on what they actually do for us.

One of the very first things I told that class was that I refused to prejudge them – it was up to them to show me what they were really like. (If you've seen the film *Dangerous Minds*, this was me doing my best impression of Michelle Pfeiffer. Teacher: 'You've all got an "A" in this subject.' Students: 'No we haven't, miss, we're all really stupid and badly behaved, hasn't anyone told you that yet?' Teacher: 'You do all have an "A" right now – it's just that it's up to you whether you hang on to it or whether you decide to throw it away.')

And somehow, somewhere along the way I managed to

'click' with the class and with Charlie. Perhaps it was that I pushed him – I believed in his ability and insisted that he stretch himself. There were some days when Charlie came into the classroom itching for a confrontation, but by trying to balance my 'hard' side with flexibility when it was needed, I somehow managed to fumble my way through. By the end of the year our lessons were full of laughter and learning (and incidentally the class had achieved really good results in their Year 9 SATs).

Sadly, Charlie was excluded from the school before he reached the end of his GCSE years. Like many kids with attitude, he refused to slot into the system and made life impossible for those teachers he didn't like or respect. Whose 'fault' it was doesn't really matter: the education system failed Charlie and all that raw ability was squandered. I wonder how Charlie turned out – perhaps his essential 'spark' was extinguished and he dropped into a life of delinquency. Or maybe, just maybe, he rose above his failed education and managed to succeed. I do hope so.

When dealing with the child who has an 'attitude', there are generally three different approaches that teachers take. Whether or not these approaches will work depends on all the typical teaching variants – the personality of the teacher and the students, the children's age, their upbringing, the ethos of the school, and so on.

Approach 1: *You have an attitude, I have an attitude, let's put them together and see who has the biggest attitude of all, shall we?*
This approach may work if you are a 'strict and scary' teacher, so long as you have good credibility with the student and probably a number of years' experience within the school. It will also help if you are over 6 foot 5, built like a rugby player and looking for a ruck. Or if you are the head teacher.

Approach 2: *You have an attitude, but I don't, so let's get all touchy-feely and try and work this out together, why don't we?*
This may be the best approach if your school is full of well-behaved and well-motivated children, who have a healthy natural respect for teachers. In many instances, though, it is the

classic first step on the slippery downward slope leading to a class full of rioting children.

Approach 3: *You have an attitude, and so do I. My attitude is that you're here to learn, because I want you to succeed. Now get on with it.* This 'take no prisoners' approach makes it clear to the child who is in charge and why it's important to defer to the teacher (not for our sake, but for *theirs*). In my experience those children who do come armed with an attitude generally respond well to this approach.

Just a final thought on this subject: teaching would be much less interesting if it weren't for the children with attitude. It's the challenge of turning these kids around that helps to stretch us as teachers. It's the toughest times that keep us on our toes and force us to constantly improve our teaching. At the very least, we should thank them for that.

A is also for . . .

Ability – How good someone is at doing something. The word 'ability' crops up a lot in teaching. From the 'low ability' child who needs lots of help, to the 'mixed ability' class where the students vary in their aptitude for the work. The mixing of abilities within a class makes life harder for the teacher, but it can be very beneficial for the students. In a 'bottom set' the weak kids might feel labelled as failures, whereas if they are in a class with more able children, the brighter ones will often pull them up.

Absence – Days where a child (or indeed teacher) is not present in school. In theory we are supposed to want every student in school at all times. In reality there are some children whose absence provokes a sigh of relief around the school.

Abuse – To treat a person or thing badly. Many teachers have been on the receiving end of abuse – both verbal and physical – from the children they teach. Having a student treat you abusively is obviously unpleasant. It is worth remembering, though, that a child who is abusive towards others will have learnt this behaviour somewhere. However hard it might be, pity rather than anger is the appropriate response. Of course, any concerns that you might have about possible child abuse must be dealt with immediately, by referring the situation to the school's CPO (Child Protection Officer).

Accelerated learning – Learning things faster. The key idea behind accelerated learning is to make maximum use of the brain; to learn how to learn better. This method is often linked to the 'multiple intelligences' identified by Howard Gardner. For more information, see www.acceleratedlearning.com. For lots of practical ideas and approaches to use in your classroom, see www.happychild.org.uk/acc/tpr/.

Acronym – Using the initial letters of words to form an abbreviated term. Teaching is absolutely stuffed full of acronyms: from AST to EBD, from DfES to PGCE. Learning how to decode these acronyms was a great puzzle to me when I first started out as a teacher. When I wasn't sure what something meant I didn't really like to ask, on the premise that I might look a bit stupid if I did. So it was that I spent most of my NQT year without a clue as to what 'AR&R' meant. This didn't matter until I was persuaded to join the 'AR&R Working Party'; at which point I was forced to confess my ignorance.

Acronyms can lead to some amusing-sounding conversations, especially when teachers combine several acronyms within one sentence, as in: 'I've been given a TA and an LSA because I'm an NQT and one of my kids has got EBD and ADHD.' 'That's good, and you should also have a chat with the SENCo, your HoD and the SMT about him in case he needs an IEP.' Do beware acronym speak, for with it comes the danger that we begin to view children via their 'labels', rather than as the complex individuals they truly are.

Administration – All the boring paperwork and organizational bits and pieces that come with the job. Considering that the main focus of the education system should be teaching and learning, the amount of administration forced upon teachers seems frankly ludicrous. Teachers wait with baited breath to see whether the Workload Agreement is actually going to cut down the amount of admin that must be done, or merely shunt it sideways into other 'new initiatives'.

AST – Advanced Skills Teacher. A career route for those teachers who are good at the job but who want to stay in the classroom rather than going down the managerial promotion path. ASTs work mainly in the classroom, but they also spend the equivalent of one day a week doing 'outreach' work (i.e. supporting other teachers or schools). It is heartening to see the talents of the 'ordinary' classroom teacher being recognized, although some people do feel that using a variable payscale is unfair and divisive. For more information, see www.standards. dfes.gov.uk/ast/ or www.teachernet.gov.uk/ast.

Advice – Going to someone for help or an opinion. The staff who work in schools are generally great at giving advice (sometimes when an opinion has not actually been requested!). We can all benefit from the advice and experience of others, whether teachers or support staff, and this is particularly important early on in our careers. On a number of occasions I have turned for advice to a colleague, and have been given practical help that has been of great benefit to me. Internet forums are a good place to ask for advice from others. Try the TES (*Times Educational Supplement*) staffroom at www.tes. co.uk/staffroom/.

Aims – What we intend the children to learn from a lesson. There can sometimes be an alarming gap between your intended aims and the actual 'learning outcomes' (the learning that really does take place). This gap is not necessarily a sign of a bad lesson plan (although Ofsted inspectors and PGCE tutors might not agree with me on that). It can instead be a sign that the teacher has been able to adapt the lesson as he or she goes along, to better suit the way the children are reacting to what has been planned. So long as they learn *something*, then surely that's a good thing?

Answer – Giving a reply to a question. Teachers spend a good deal of time asking questions and (hopefully) getting answers from their children. If you face the irritation of five different kids shouting out what they think, there is a very simple answer to your problem. Rather than saying 'Who can tell me the answer?', instead ask 'Put your hand up if you can tell me ...' By doing this you will very quickly train your children to respond in the way you require.

Apology – Saying sorry when you've made a mistake. As a teacher it can be tempting to feel that you must never be seen to get it wrong. However, we are bound to make mistakes from time to time. Be willing to apologize when you treat a child or class badly, or if you make an error during your delivery of a lesson. This shows your students that you are human underneath it all (despite the evidence to the contrary).

Assembly – A large school gathering, typically held in the assembly hall. Assemblies vary widely in their content and appeal. From the traditional head teacher-led meeting, to the more modern assembly in which the children play an active part. If asked to prepare an assembly with your class or form group, make sure that you hand over the reins to the students as far as possible. Encourage their input into planning and delivery, and then stand aside to watch.

Assessment – Checking to see how much the students have learned. Good assessment will help the teacher monitor the children's progress and plan for future teaching and learning. Assessment can be both formal (tests, exams) and informal (making your own mental notes about how the students are doing). As I now know (see 'Acronym' above), assessment forms the 'A' of the 'AR&R' trio: 'Assessment, Recording and Reporting'.

BEHAVIOUR

To act in a specific way.

For many teachers, getting behaviour right is the number one worry in their classrooms. Controlling a class of thirty or more children is never going to be easy or straightforward, even if the children are inclined to behave well. Ask the typical 'man on the street' if he fancies an hour in front of a bunch of snotty five-year-olds or hormonal teenagers, and watch him quake with fear. That we somehow manage to get our students to behave, and to actually learn something as well, should be a cause for celebration and a source of pride.

The thing about behaviour is that if you can get it right, your classroom feels like a fantastic place. The children are all able to learn, there's a great feeling of achievement and success in the air, and you don't have to waste your energy on dealing with misbehaviour. Although it feels great to have a class completely under control, getting good behaviour is not about self-gratification for the teacher. The only real reason that we have to demand good behaviour is so that quality learning can take place. And when it does happen you find yourself actually able to get on with the teaching – this is how the job can and should be.

On the other hand, if you do lose control of a class, whether momentarily or on a long-term basis, it makes you feel sick to the stomach. The classroom turns from a place of positive achievement into a prison of frustration – both for the teacher who cannot actually do any teaching, and also for those students who do wish to work. And as you watch the children doing exactly what they want, you just know that this is the day when the head teacher will decide to pay an impromptu visit.

When we have to face a class full of poorly behaved kids, it's tempting for us to blame our own skill as teachers. In fact, classroom behaviour depends on a whole range of factors. Many of the reasons why your children mess you around are actually outside your direct control. The causes might be linked to a poor school ethos, a hopelessly large number of children with behavioural special needs in the class, the 'baggage' that your students bring in from outside the school gates, and so on and on.

As a so-called 'behaviour expert', people often ask me whether I think children's behaviour has deteriorated in recent times, and if so, why this might be. I'm not a great fan of the 'good old days' philosophy of life, in which society is on a downward spiral and where things were always better in the past. Personally, though, my feeling is that behaviour probably has deteriorated, and that this is down to a number of different causes. Some of these causes are things that we could do something about, if the people who made the decisions in education would only listen to what teachers really need. Some of the causes are far wider-ranging, and would require a sea change in our society to alter.

In recent years our children have been increasingly empowered to say what they do and do not want. Although this brings with it some downsides, overall it is surely a good thing. As a young child, I spent a whole year refusing to go to school. Although my 'school phobia' (as it's now called) had a variety of complex reasons behind it, one of the main factors was a visceral fear of a number of the teachers at my school. The days when many teachers were terrifyingly 'strict and scary' are now, thankfully, behind us. This teaching style may well work for some, but for the quiet and fearful kids, it can be enough to put them off school for life.

So, why is it that the behaviour we face in the classroom is getting worse, apparently with each passing day? Much has to do, in my opinion, with dictates from above. The government wouldn't dream of telling doctors how to practise medicine, but they are only too willing to tell teachers how to teach. Although in theory the current policy of inclusion is a great idea, for it not to simply fail, for both children and teachers, it has to be put into place properly. At the moment teachers do not receive enough support or training to cope with a small number of severely damaged children. These are the children whose psychological needs go far beyond what we can possibly hope to manage in a large group situation. By putting them in the mainstream classroom, and having to cope with the subsequent behavioural problems, all we are doing is failing everyone. There are some students who are far better suited to life in a specialist school, where small classes and experienced teachers are better able to meet their needs.

The curriculum is another bone of contention when it comes to difficult behaviour. As it stands at the moment, we're being asked to teach a curriculum that doesn't suit a good number of the children in our schools. A narrow curriculum is bound to lead to difficult behaviour if it has little connection with the outside world, and if it doesn't offer chances for the less academically able to succeed.

The supposed system of 'parental choice' and its best friend the 'league tables' are also a source of problems. Instead of greater choice for all, they have merely led to a choice for those who have the power to push for what they want, or the money to buy a home in the right catchment area. This has meant an increasing divide between those schools that succeed and those that don't. Consequently there are some schools in which the sheer weight of numbers of poorly motivated children becomes infectious. If you are a 'failing' child in a 'failing' school it is hardly surprising that you might turn your anger onto the teachers.

Of course, outside influences are also at work when it comes to behaviour. The children of today are bombarded by violent images on television and in other forms of the media – it surely follows that this has at least some influence on children's behaviour. The excessive use of television and computer games seems to have led to a generation of children who simply cannot concentrate unless they are given overt stimulation. I've no problem making my lessons more interactive and interesting, but are we not in danger of losing the power of true imagination and the vital skill of concentration?

There is also a feeling these days that rewards should come easily. Our children see footballers making millions of pounds by exploiting their skill; or drug dealers driving brand new flashy cars. If it comes easy to them, then is it any surprise that our children feel that the world owes them a living? We also have to contend with the negative image in society as a whole of what teachers and schools can offer. This is compounded by the total lack of trust in us as professionals from the government, the press and parents. Another culprit is poor parenting skills – the fact that some of our children come to school with very little idea about how to behave.

Behaviour management is a complex issue: even in my book *Getting the Buggers to Behave* (Continuum, 2001), there was only space to scratch the surface. So much is about the teacher's ability to manage each individual situation. In teaching, no two instances are the same, and what works in one scenario may well fail in another. There is no magic wand that anyone can wave to get your children to behave. On the other hand there are some very general tips that will work for you most of the time.

Being a good behaviour manager is about the ability to balance complete certainty and confidence in yourself and your demands ('this is exactly what I want and I am certain that I will get it') alongside an equal amount of flexibility ('I know when I must bend rather than break; I accept that sometimes there is no point in pushing an issue'). Set high expectations of what your children can achieve – believe in them and the power of their potential, no matter how much they try to drag your expectations down. Always remember that managing behaviour is never about win or lose – it's not us against them, it's us against all the things that stand between them and a decent education. Try to stay positive as far as you possibly can (this can be incredibly hard with the nightmare classes). Finally, do learn to put yourself in your children's shoes, seeing yourself and your lessons from their perspective.

B is also for . . .

Bad – Nasty, naughty, the opposite of good. The word 'bad' is fast disappearing from the world of education, particularly when used in connection with behaviour, where the words 'difficult' or 'challenging' should be used instead. Although some might see this as an example of political correctness gone mad, there is in fact a good reason to make the distinction. The problem with saying a child's behaviour is 'bad' is that this suggests that the child him/herself is a 'bad' person. Our aim should be to label the behaviour instead. So it is that behaviour becomes 'difficult' or 'challenging'.

Bag – A flexible container for carrying stuff around. In the distant past when I was educated, children had desks with lift up tops where they could store their equipment, or alternatively were given lockers in which to keep their things. The constraints of space and money mean that there are less and less schools with lockers. As a teacher you will regularly see children carting around huge bags of stuff, particularly in the secondary school. Your first thought might be for their physical health – it can't be good for their poor backs! Your second thought will be to wonder why, with such huge school bags, they still have to ask whether they can borrow a pen.

Blazer – A jacket worn at school, typically decorated with a school crest. The wearing of blazers usually indicates that a school is (or the head thinks it is) an old-fashioned place with an emphasis on correct uniform and other high standards.

Bluff – Pretending that something is true when it isn't. In my opinion a big part of the art of being a teacher is to do with the ability to bluff convincingly. This is particularly so when it comes to behaviour management. There is no real reason why a class of thirty young people should do what the teacher says.

Much of the compliance that we do receive is connected to the 'role' that we play as teachers.

I have used the art of bluff with great success on a number of occasions. With one particularly difficult class, who simply refused to be silent and listen to me, I set up a video camera in the corner of the classroom. Of course they quickly asked why I was filming them (sample amusing comment: 'You can't film us, it's an infringement of our human rights'). I explained I had told the head teacher how difficult the class was being, and that he had asked me to video them so he could see who the culprits were. The head teacher very kindly came in to support my bluff. Of course he didn't actually have to watch the video – with this promise hanging over them they soon started to behave themselves.

There are several key factors in creating a successful bluff. Firstly, link your pretence closely to something that might actually be true. Secondly, ensure that your bluff is one where the children can't risk that you might be telling the truth (in the scenario above: 'she might be lying but we can't take the chance that the head teacher might actually see what we're doing'). You will also need to look so convincing that the children do not dare to 'call' your bluff, keeping a totally straight face at all times.

Body language – The 'language' of our bodies – conscious and subconscious positions or movements that communicate a message to others. Teachers are able to 'say' a whole heap of stuff without even opening their mouths. Like actors we convey many subtle and not so subtle messages by the use of clear body language. Being able to control children through body language takes time and experience. When it comes to body language, it is often a good idea to overdo the message by 'hamming it up' for the class.

Boffin – A term used to describe academic and hard-working students. Being a boffin is, sadly, not considered a positive attribute in many schools. At break times boffins will tend to congregate together, often in the school library, probably on the basis that there is safety in numbers.

Borrow – Making a loan of something from another person. 'Can I borrow a pen?' is one of those requests that scores highly on the 'things that irritate teachers' scale. This puts the teacher in a bind, though, because without a pen the children have an excuse not to do their work. Before I knew any better, I used to happily 'loan' out biros to my students. Of course, once I realized that I was rapidly depleting the EEC Pen Mountain, I knocked that one on the head.

There are various ways of dealing with the pen borrowing request and the subsequent loss of loaned out pens. 'I don't have any pens, they've all been nicked by you lot, so you'll have to borrow one off a friend' is one possible response. Alternatively, if you have the luxury of pens with lids, then hang on to these lids and at least you will know how many pens you are due back at the end of the lesson. On a more imaginative note, a teacher once suggested a great idea to me. This was to have a selection of really girly pens in your classroom (ones with pink fluffy bits on them – the shop 'Claire's Accessories' is the place to get these). When a student asks to borrow a pen (and it's frequently a boy), then offer him one of your fluffy creations. This will be enough to put him off asking again 99 per cent of the time, and even if he does accept your offer, you will easily be able to spot your pen to get it back.

Of course, teachers are also notorious for 'borrowing' things without any intention of actually effecting the return of said items. I sometimes look back on the amount of mugs that I have lost in the course of my teaching career. They provide a sobering reflection of the way that the original meaning of the word 'borrow' has been somewhat lost.

Boundaries – The limits within which we ask our children to stay. The failure to set adequate boundaries in the home (see 'Behaviour' above) is, to my mind, one of the main reasons why we experience such difficulty in getting our little angels to behave themselves. I like to use the image of a box to help describe boundaries. The idea is that we offer our children a large box within the confines of which anything goes. Inside the box are behaviours such as using appropriate language, treating others with respect, working to the best of their ability, and so on. Outside the box are all the things we don't want them to do.

It's only natural for our children to push at the edges of the box to see if they can stretch the limits a bit. The hard thing for the teacher is deciding when to say 'stop!' Clearly, calling the teacher a 'f****** b******' is way outside the box, but other more subtle misdemeanours mean we must constantly make judgement calls about where the edges of our boundaries lie.

Brain Gym® – Using specific physical movements to improve learning and to encourage a student to use both sides of his or her brain. Brain Gym style activities can usefully be incorporated into lessons to break up longer periods of focused work (and they're also a lot of fun). Here's an example of a useful physical exercise: put your right hand on the left side of your nose, and your left hand on your right cheek. Now swap the two over (it's hard at first), gradually increasing the speed. For more information about this approach, see www.braingym. org and www.braingym.org.uk.

Break time – A rest period in which the students play games, consume junk foods, hide in the library, or visit the toilets to smoke. In theory, it is also a time when the teachers might take a break to have a coffee, read the paper, or have a chat with their friends. In reality, many teachers do work through their breaks, in the knowledge that the work that must be done will still be there when the school bell rings at the end of the day.

Ironically, the way that breaks are structured within the school day does not actually lead to the best quality learning. Research has shown that for maximum concentration, we learn best in blocks of around fifteen to twenty minutes. Where formal break times come up to three hours apart, it is a good idea for the teacher to include his or her own informal breaks within a lesson. In a desk-bound lesson this might mean incorporating some 'stretch times', where the children can simply get up and have a walk around. It could mean using some more formalized ideas for breaks, such as the Brain Gym® activities described above.

Bullying – Repeated, negative and undesired treatment of a victim(s) by one or more others. Bullying comes in many different forms: it can be physical, verbal, psychological or social. Sadly, bullying is almost inevitable when you place a large group of people in an enclosed environment such as a school. The 'herd instinct', in which we blindly follow the majority will, means that the weak, the strange or those who are outsiders for some reason may get a hard time. Happily, the impact of bullying is increasingly being recognized, and schools are taking steps to minimize the damage. Bullying is something that can affect staff as well as children. For more information, see www.childline.org.uk/Bullying.asp and www.bullying.co.uk.

IS FOR . . .

CHAIR

A piece of furniture on which to sit.

Although we rarely think about them, chairs are actually an important feature of school life. Perhaps we have come to take them for granted because they are so ubiquitous. From the tiny doll like chairs of the primary classroom, to the brown plastic chairs covered in tippexed graffiti and old chewing gum that feature in secondary schools. Chairs can, on occasions, be the stuff of nightmares: the chair wielded above a child's head as he threatens revenge against a teacher who has dared to lay down the law.

Teachers have to fight a constant battle to try and ensure correct chair usage. Many children seem to find it almost impossible to sit properly, tipping back on their chairs repeatedly instead (my mum used to call this 'cockling your chair'). In an attempt to curb this practice, teachers will often tell the class horrific stories about how a friend of a friend's auntie's cousin used to know someone who knew someone who had tipped back on his chair too far, and ended up with a broken back. In my experience, this has little impact on the chair-cocklers, who continue to throw caution to the wind by engaging in constant chair tipping. Haven't they heard of risk assessment?

In some classes, the ability to actually sit down on a chair is missing. You wouldn't imagine that it was a particularly difficult skill to master, but it must be harder than it looks, because some of our students seem to find it nigh on impossible. This inability can lead to a classroom of children wandering around the room rather than staying in their seats. In some instances, I have taught in classrooms that look like a mass game of musical chairs. One of our key aims, then, must be to teach children how to sit down properly. (Perhaps a 'National Sitting-in-Chair Strategy' might be in order?)

Teachers get chairs too, of course, although in many classrooms they are rarely used for sitting on (we're far too busy rushing around the room trying to curb that 'challenging' behaviour). I'm a great fan of the technique of standing on a chair (or indeed desk) to teach, in the style of Robin Williams in *Dead Poets Society*. This forces your children to see you from a different angle or perspective, although it is not recommended if you are wearing a short skirt.

In the staffroom, the chair features in many classic school anecdotes. The 'I wouldn't sit there if I were you' scenario, as the unsuspecting NQT goes to rest her bottom on Mr Smith's chair. Chairs can also become a way of marking out territory. They define the areas where the young and trendy gather to compare notes on the previous night's pub crawl, or the old and grizzled meet to share complaints about the youth of today.

When a number of chairs are gathered together in one place (whether classroom, staff meeting or training session) the choice that people make about where to sit provides a great indicator of their attitude. Those in the back row are the rebels, who are hoping to get away with messing around or doing some marking. Those who sit at the front are the keenos who have all the answers.

A final thought on the subject of chairs. As I sit here writing this book, my posterior is parked on an ergonomically designed chair, adjusted to exactly the correct level for me to type comfortably, safely and efficiently. Even so, I find that after about half an hour, I am itching to get up and walk around. The chairs we offer to our children are rarely of decent quality. Obviously cost is a factor, but if we expect our children to stay seated for all or most of the day, it surely follows that we might think to offer them a comfy seat on which to sit?

C is also for ...

Caretaker – Typically a gruff but kind-hearted man who keeps the school buildings running. It is a good idea to make at least a passing acquaintance with the caretaker. When the radiator in your room spouts a leak, or when you need some chairs set out for an assembly, you will need him (or her) on your side.

Certainty – Knowing exactly what you want. It's my belief that a teacher's ability to look certain in front of a class is a vital skill in effective classroom management. Certainty helps you appear more in control of your classroom and gives the children a sense of security in your presence. Your high levels of certainty will manifest themselves in a complete clarity about your expectations and a confident and competent exterior appearance. In theory, your certainty should be rewarded with a class of children doing exactly as you ask. In reality, there will be times when no one does as you say.

Certificate – A document given to acknowledge achievement. Rather sweetly, many children seem to be inordinately proud about receiving a certificate. This is perhaps more to do with what the certificate represents ('we're really proud of you and what you've achieved') than what it actually is (a sheet of paper with some words of praise on it). I was once awarded a certificate myself, which takes pride of place in my 'portfolio' of nice things that kids have given me. It was an award from the Year 11 students in my first school, given just before the end of their GCSE year. They had voted me 'Favourite Female Teacher'. Despite the fact that the award was addressed to Miss Cowly (my spelling strategies obviously didn't work that well, then), the glow of achievement still warms my heart to this day.

Challenging – As in 'I teach in a challenging school'. This euphemism is teacher-speak for either: (a) 'I am an educational martyr who loves working with really tough kids and I won't hear a word said against them', or (b) 'I teach a bunch of psychotic maniacs and I'm planning to escape from this hellhole as soon as I possibly can.'

Chewing gum – A sweet chewy substance that is kept in the mouth rather than swallowed. Many schools wage a constant battle against chewing gum. Although it can seem petty, the problem with the stuff is not so much when it's in the child's mouth, as when it gets stuck on seats, carpets, hair, etc. (A quick tip – there are various chemicals that can be used to get gum off your clothes, but in fact putting them in the freezer will make removal simple and easy.) Picking up on gum chewing in your classroom can make a strong statement about your attitude as a teacher. There are two approaches that you might take: (a) insisting that every child caught with gum puts it in the bin immediately, or (b) with older students, making it clear that you have noticed the gum chewing, but agreeing to 'overlook' it in return for hard work. If you do decide to wander the classroom with a bin, looking for offenders, whatever you do don't say 'spit'. Your students will most likely take you literally and you will end up with a bin full of frothy gobs.

CPO – Child Protection Officer. A senior member of staff within a school will act as the designated CPO, responsible for the safety and welfare of the children. If you have any concerns about the welfare of a child whom you teach, then find out who the CPO is at your school, and pass the matter on to him or her.

Children – Young people, plural of child. Children don't get to be children for very long these days. (Adult concerns seem very quickly to arrive – make-up, fashion, boy/girlfriends, etc.) When I think back to my own childhood, I have vivid memories of freedom, of playing in the streets without fear of strangers. These days, the desire to protect our children from risk means they are cosseted away from any potential sources of harm.

For teachers, children are (or at least, should be) what it is all about. It's the beauty contestant's cliché about wanting to work with animals and children, but for real. There are so many wonderful things about children. They have such a powerful sense of wonder about life. They have a quest, a real thirst, for knowledge about the world in which they live. They have a great sense of imagination and can use play both to have fun and to learn as well. Children are not yet cynical about the world, although this cynicism seems to arrive younger and younger.

We owe it to our children to protect and care for them. There are lots of children who do not get the start in life that they deserve. It does make me angry when I meet and work with children who have been mistreated by their parents. (Although it's always worth remembering that people who are bad parents were most likely poorly treated children themselves.) However, as teachers we must accept that we can't take on the woes of every individual child; you'd go mad if you tried to do that.

It's really important that we never forget what it was like to be a child. Being able to sit in your children's shoes, and see things from their perspective, will help you understand when things are going wrong in your classroom. If we ask our children to sit and listen silently for more than ten minutes, then we can expect some resistance. If we set work that is boring to the point of sleep, then again we can expect them to put up a fight. Being able to see your teaching from the viewpoint of the children will help you to solve any problems that crop up.

Choice – Making a decision between two or more things. Using 'choice' is a very powerful technique in managing behaviour. The idea is to pass responsibility for the behaviour over to the child – you can't force someone to behave, but if they are asked to make the decision for themselves, they are far more likely to comply. If a student is misbehaving, try giving him or her the following offer: 'You have a choice. You can either stop doing x, get on with your work, and see if you can earn a merit by the end of the lesson. Alternatively, you can continue to do x, but I'm afraid you will have to accept the consequences, which are y and z.'

Circle time – Time spent working as a whole class, using the format of a circle. The 'circle time' approach was originally written about by Jenny Mosley (for more information, see www.circle-time.co.uk). There are lots of positive outcomes to be had from circle work, including team building, improved cooperation and the development of oral skills. The great thing about working in a circle is that it means that everyone can see and hear everyone else easily. It is a very democratic format – it suggests that 'we are all equal, we are all sharing this experience'.

As a drama teacher, I've had a lot of experience in using circles, and the following 'top tips' will stand you in good stead for using them in your own classroom. First of all, make sure that you get the shape right – it might sound petty, but a circle that is exactly circular suggests that the teacher has high standards and expectations. Working in a circle can put pressure on those students who find it hard to contribute. Try not to put your children on the spot – make some sort of provision for them to 'pass' if they don't want to join in the activity.

If you have problems with your children calling out in the circle, then using a 'conch' is a great idea. This is an important looking item (a beautiful shell, a stick with beads and feathers) which allows the holder to speak without interruption. Finally, don't be too predictable when using circles. The natural inclination for right-handers is always to go clockwise and to start with the child standing to our left. Counter this by sometimes going anticlockwise, and sometimes starting with a child from the middle of the circle.

Coat – An outer garment, worn to keep warm. Some students seem to have an unhealthy attachment to their coats (as though they are the equivalent of the 'comfort blanket' that a young child insists on keeping to hand). When I do supply teaching, it always amazes me how many children are supposedly 'allowed' to wear their coats in class.

Coffee – A hot drink made from coffee beans, high in caffeine. The fuel that keeps our schools and teachers going.

Coffee-breath – The smell of a coffee-fuelled teacher's breath that can floor a child at a hundred paces.

Colleagues – The currently popular term for the other people who work at your school. The politically correct tenor of this term suggests that 'we're all in this together'.

Communication – Sharing information with other people. At its heart, all teaching is about communication: the teacher communicating with the children, the children communicating with each other and with the teacher. We can communicate both directly and in many more subtle (and often subconscious) ways. We might simply be talking to the class about the work or about what we want from them. However, it is worth remembering that we will also communicate a great deal about our state of mind by the way that we hold our bodies and the way that our voices actually sound.

Concentration – The ability to focus on one thing to the exclusion of all others. It takes time and plenty of practice to develop concentration, and many of our children start school with very little skill in this area. However, concentration is vital if our students are going to learn properly. It will always be more difficult for your children to concentrate when there are lots of distractions in the room, so if possible aim to have some quiet working time during each lesson. There are plenty of ways that you can actually teach and develop concentration within your classroom. Using simple forms of meditative activity will be very beneficial; for instance asking the students to close their eyes and simply listen to the sounds inside and outside the room for a couple of minutes. Focus exercises are widely used within drama lessons, so you might like to ask any drama specialists in your school for ideas. For some useful advice on developing concentration, see www.kent.ac.uk/uelt/learning/online/concentr-tips.html.

Confidence – A belief in yourself and in what you do. The best teachers radiate confidence and this helps the children to feel secure in their presence. This feeling of inner belief is closely linked to self-esteem. The more positive that you can feel about yourself and what you can do, the more confident you will become. If you're naturally shy in social situations, like me, then it's worth remembering you don't actually have to be confident, you just have to *appear* to be so.

Confrontation – To argue or fight with someone. A small number of children will exhibit extremely confrontational attitudes, which have most likely been picked up at home. Although there will be times when you need to 'put your foot down' with these children, overall it is best to avoid confrontation if at all possible. Do bear in mind that once a child gets locked into a confrontation, it can be very difficult for him or her to pull out of that frame of mind. Confrontation is hard to maintain without the 'fuel' of a response, so you might try letting the child blow off steam for a while, ensuring that he or she is safe, and not likely to harm others.

Conscientious – Taking great care over work, a very focused and hard-working approach. The word 'conscientious' is often used to describe the 'model' child, especially in a written report (it sounds fancy and covers a multitude of attributes).

Consistency – Doing the same thing in the same way every time. It is important for teachers to respond in the same way to the same behaviours every time they happen, as this helps the children know where they stand. Consistency across the school is the 'holy grail' of behaviour management policies, particularly for secondary head teachers. What they want is for the children to receive the same expectations and the same high standards from every teacher. Of course, teachers being unique individuals who run their classrooms in their own personal ways, consistency is actually very hard to achieve.

Cover – Taking someone else's lesson because they are absent from school. There are a number of different approaches to the taking of cover lessons. Some teachers will write the work on the board, say 'get on with it' and sit down to do some marking. Other teachers will make an effort to actually teach the work that has been set. When setting cover for drama lessons I had a great deal of sympathy. With no chairs or tables in the room, classroom management becomes a tricky task.

Creativity – The ability to devise an original idea. In the educational world creativity is a bit of a 'hot topic' at the moment. The overly prescribed nature of the curriculum has left little room for children to flex their creativity muscles. So it is that creativity becomes yet another thing that we're meant to fit into the crowded school day. Bizarrely, this rather goes against the nature of the beast: to be creative requires a lack of rules and a willingness to get it wrong.

Curriculum – The subjects that are studied at school. The 'powers that be' who decide on the content and delivery of the school curriculum are making some crucial decisions that shape the way we educate our children. There are so many choices to be made – which subjects are most important, how should they be taught, how do we fit them all in, how do we divide up the different subjects?

When it comes to the curriculum, there can be a tendency to accept the way things are. Perhaps we don't question the curriculum often enough (probably because of a sense that we don't have any power to change it). I taught overseas for a while, and was lucky enough to teach within the International Baccalaureate system, which offers a very different curriculum, both in content and delivery.

DIFFERENTIATION

Adapting the way that you teach to suit each individual child.

The idea behind differentiation – that every individual child will learn best at a different level and in a different way – is one with which all teachers would happily agree. In one corner of the Reception classroom is Jimmy, who arrived at school this year barely able to speak. In the other corner is Serena, who turned up with her well-thumbed copy of *The Wind in the Willows*, demanding to know when the class would be beginning their study of Shakespearean literature. Of course these children have differing needs when it comes to deciding how and what to teach them!

In reality, though, individual differentiation is one of those great ideas in teaching that seem to fall apart in the face of the realities of the school system. Although we would all dearly love to suit our teaching to each individual child, this just isn't possible within the constraints of the 24 hours that are available in each day (we have to sleep and eat at some point). If teachers were given classes of only five children, they would happily differentiate for each one of them. Unfortunately, with up to thirty (or more) children in the average class, differentiation is bound to be a bit hit and miss.

The differentiation that you actually manage to do can take place in a range of different ways. You might differentiate for one or more individuals, you could differentiate the work given to different groups, you might differentiate the type of work offered to a whole class. Differentiation can be 'by task' – giving different activities to different children, or it might be 'by support' – i.e. allocating a child additional help, for instance from a Learning Support Assistant (LSA). We might be adapting the content of what we teach, or looking at different 'learning styles', or perhaps even altering the classroom environment to better suit our individual learners.

As with many things in teaching, if an idea isn't working exactly as intended we just rename it to make sure that no one realizes. So it is that differentiation can also take place by 'outcome'. In plain English, all that this term means is that when you set the whole class the same task, they will differentiate it for themselves by producing different standards and amounts of work. Although we might manage to adapt the work to suit those learners at the top or bottom ends of the spectrum, in reality many lessons will feature work that is differentiated simply by the outcome that is reached.

Learning styles are an integral part of the whole subject of differentiation. The idea is that children learn best using one of three main 'styles' – visual, auditory or kinaesthetic. So now, on top of differentiating the content of the work for each of our children, we should also aim to adapt our lesson to suit their learning styles. Again, give me those five children (and the freedom to adapt the curriculum as I see fit), and I will gladly suit it to each one.

In reality, the most realistic way for teachers to suit their lessons to each child is to incorporate a range of different teaching methods and learning styles within each lesson. So it is that part of the lesson appeals to the visual learners, part to the auditory and part to the kinaesthetic.

For a detailed outline of what differentiation is, and links to lots of sites that look at the subject, see www.greenfield.durham. sch.uk/differentiation.htm.

D is also for...

Deadly stare – A pointed gaze used by the teacher to make a child or class behave. This is the classic non-verbal signal, mastered by most teachers in their first year on the job. Without the need for words, the 'deadly stare' tells a class or an individual: 'If you don't stop doing that immediately you are likely to suffer in the most horrible way known to humankind.' A word of warning – take care when unleashing your deadly stare in public. You will probably be able to win every Tube train staring competition going. However, the day might come when an innocent member of the public mistakes your icy glare for an indication that they have their own personal stalker.

Delegate – Passing work on to someone else. The skill of delegation is one that teachers should learn early on, to ease the pressure of workload. Many managers will of course happily delegate their more loathsome tasks to you. The skill of successful delegation is to 'big up' the person to whom you are delegating. Make him or her feel that you have singled them out for this task because they are so skilful at this particular activity.

There are many classroom tasks that can be delegated to the children. I'm very keen on the technique of 'you be teacher', in which the children are asked to deliver a small part of the lesson, or to take on some of the work of the teacher. To my mind, this technique offers a great way of giving responsibility to children, particularly those who normally seek attention in more negative ways. 'Being teacher' is viewed by most children as a great reward. It can also be very instructive for them about the difficulties of being a teacher, showing them that your job is not quite as straightforward as they might think. (For a cheap laugh, ask one of your children to try writing in a straight line on the whiteboard.)

Department – A collection of subject specialists who teach within the same group of subjects in a secondary school.

DfES – The Department for Education and Skills, the government body overseeing education in English state schools (www.dfes.gov.uk). For Wales, see www.learning.wales.gov.uk, for Northern Ireland see www.deni.gov.uk, for Scotland see www.ltscotland.org.uk.

Desks – Tables at which the children sit to do their work. I'm a great believer in the power of sitting on desks – both myself when talking to the class, and also in the sense of informality given when the kids sit on the desks themselves for a class discussion. In the 'good old days', desks were typically made of wood with a lift up lid, where you could store your equipment and books, and under which (in a class with an unobservant teacher) you could sneakily read your favourite comic. The wooden surfaces of these desks also made a wonderful surface on which to scratch your name for all posterity: 'I woz ere' being a favoured phrase of the graffiti artist. Be warned if you plan to move some desks around: these days, the undersides of the metal/plastic tables are likely to feature globs of ancient chewing gum, which will affix themselves to the unsuspecting teacher's hand.

Detention – Removing free time from a student: typically at break or lunch time, or after school. If your children have a tendency not to turn up to the detentions that you set, your working life can become an escalating game of 'cat and mouse' with your non-attendees. In the past, I have foolishly set a five minute after-school detention, which on the child's failure to appear turned into a twenty minute detention, then up to half an hour, an hour, and so on and on. Eventually, with the threat of a five hour Saturday detention in front of the deputy head, the child turned up sheepishly at my door. 'But I can't even remember why you gave me that detention in the first place, miss.'

Displays – Work mounted on the classroom or corridor walls in an artistic fashion. Displays can range from wallpaper to cover the cracks in the classroom walls to a celebration of what your children are learning in your classroom. A wonderful array of displays will magically appear in the days before a school 'open evening'. Of course, the Workload Agreement means that we are no longer meant to be responsible for putting up displays. Personally, I find this slightly sad, because devising displays is a fun and creative part of the job. If you are still having to put up your own displays, and you want to save your time and energy, then get the children involved, and give yourself the job title of 'artistic director'.

Duty – Supervision of the students by the teacher outside of lesson times. See 'Frustrations' for some comments on this wonderful aspect of our job.

EXPECTATIONS

What we want (or hope to get) from our children.

I can still remember my lecturers at university going on and on about the importance of expectations, but it took me a good few years of teaching to really understand what they meant. Now I see that expectations are vital because they allow you to look like you know exactly what you want, and consequently to appear confident, certain and in control. And once you achieve this, your students get the feeling that you are in charge of the way that your classroom runs. This gives them a great sense of security.

The problem is that, when you first go into teaching, you honestly don't know what you expect from your classes. In fact, you probably don't know what you're actually 'allowed' to expect from them either, or indeed what they will expect from you. If you're as old as me, you might have an image from your own school days of children sitting silently in rows and standing up when the teacher enters the room. Is it still like this, you wonder on your first teaching practice, or will they want to wander the room and talk while I'm speaking?

Some expectations are fairly straightforward to work out. When Danny tells you with a poker face that their previous teacher allowed them to wear their coats and use their mobiles in class, you can be damn sure that he's having you on. But if honest-looking Sammy tells you that their last teacher let them go to lunch five minutes early, because of a group of bullies in the year above, then you might be a bit less certain about whether this is really allowed.

Nobody can actually tell you what your expectations should be. There are so many factors that will play a part in working out what you want, including:

- your own personal opinions about what should and shouldn't be allowed;
- your age, upbringing and previous experiences;
- the school's requirements of work and behaviour;
- the age of the children you teach;
- the personalities and home backgrounds of the children you teach;
- the 'ethos' of your school;
- the local and street culture of your area.

For some teachers in some schools, hearing a teenager say 'f***' if he bangs against a desk will be completely unacceptable. Other teachers in a different situation might feel that turning a 'blind ear' and just letting it ride is the best way to go.

Being a really effective teacher is about the ability to balance clarity and certainty of expectations with the flexibility to adapt these expectations as the situation requires. While our expectations need to be clear and certain, they must also change according to the circumstances. If Annie turns up in the foulest of foul moods one day, determined to make trouble, you are hardly going to succeed with her if you insist on rigid obedience of every rule. Your expectations will also need to be adapted during the school year. Although they must be set up clearly at the start, you may find it possible to pull back slightly as you go along.

While we're on the subject of expectations, it's worth also thinking about what our children expect from us. When we first start out as teachers, it's tempting to believe that the students expect us to be their friend. This is the slippery first step on the downward slope to Misbehaviour City. What children most definitely don't want is a teacher who is 'down with them'. Remember how embarrassing it was when you were a child, and an adult tried to act youthful and cool? Instead, your children probably expect you to be slightly removed from them – an adult role model who sets high standards for work and behaviour, although not necessarily in an authoritarian way. They probably wouldn't mind you being a bit 'cool' and having a token interest in modern culture. But it's probably not a good idea to admit your love for hip hop and texting if you are over thirty – that's simply beyond the pale for most children.

E is also for ...

EAZ – Education Action Zone. These 'zones' involve the building of local partnerships between schools, parents, the community, businesses and local authorities. See www. standards.dfes.gov.uk/eaz/ for more information.

EBD – Emotional and Behavioural Difficulties. A generic term for children with behavioural special needs.

Engage – To capture the interest. Being able to engage our children in their work is surely the aim of every teacher. Students who are truly engaged in their learning will work hard without any thought of messing around. There are many ways in which you can improve levels of engagement in your classroom. By its nature, school is an artificial environment, removed from the 'real world'. This can cause feelings of 'it's not relevant' in relation to the work. To counter this, make the work relevant and exciting. You might bring in some interesting props to begin the lesson; or you could provide a fictional scenario and get the children to work within this fiction to make the learning feel 'real'.

There are many benefits for the teacher in delivering engaging lessons. For a start, you will get a wonderful reputation (particularly useful in the secondary school, where you will be meeting large numbers of different children, who discuss their teachers outside the classroom). You will also gain a sense of personal satisfaction if your lessons are fun to teach.

Of course, the requirements of the curriculum will sometimes get in the way of exciting lessons. There are some subjects that you will have to teach in a straightforward and fairly boring way. However, if you typically offer your children engaging and exciting lessons, then you can refer to this generosity when you do have to slog through the dull bits. Although you might feel that planning and delivering engaging lessons sounds like too much hard work, it doesn't actually have to be at all tiring to keep up the levels of interest. With high levels of motivation it will often be possible for you to hand over the reins to the children and let them practically run the lesson themselves.

Enjoy – To take pleasure in something. There are many reasons why being a teacher can and should be an enjoyable experience. Unlike many jobs, no two days (in fact, no two minutes) will be the same. We get the chance to see our children learning and developing, we have the opportunity to be creative and inspirational in what we do, and we get the chance to actually make a real difference to somebody else's life. The children can easily sense when they have a teacher who genuinely enjoys his or her work, and they will typically respond to this enjoyment by feeling more positive themselves.

Enthusiasm – A key attribute for teachers, particularly strong in newcomers to the profession (some of the old hands will have run out of it years ago). Being enthusiastic about teaching is obviously important, but realistically it can be hard to maintain under all the pressures of the job. Be a little wary of the standard job advertisement request for a teacher with enthusiasm, as this can on occasions be code for 'a teacher onto whom we can dump all those extra jobs that nobody else has the time/energy/stupidity to agree to do'.

Equipment – The tools or clothing needed to do specific work. Children who 'forget' their equipment can drive the teacher to distraction. In subjects where bringing the correct kit is a key feature (for instance, PE) the teacher will need to decide how to cope with the issue of forgotten equipment. Offering a manky set of unfashionable (but obviously clean) kit is one very strong incentive for children to remember their clothes.

Ethos – The beliefs and relationships within an organization. This nebulous concept helps to identify the overall 'feel' of a school. If you imagine your school as a living creature, the school ethos would be that creature's personality. The ethos of a school can change alarmingly quickly – both from good to bad and vice versa. An effective and respected head teacher could be seen to represent the head of the creature, while all the other staff, and also the children, act as its body and limbs.

Euphemism – Using a soft expression in place of a plain-spoken one. Teaching is stuffed full of euphemisms – no one seems to want to call a spade a spade in the world of education!

Evaluate – To judge the quality of something. We spend plenty of time evaluating what our children produce for us, but evaluation can also be a really valuable tool for the teacher in improving the quality of our work. The truly reflective teacher will learn how to evaluate everything that he or she does in the classroom, literally on a moment to moment basis. When something appears not to be working (whether your manage-ment of behaviour or the lesson that you are teaching) then try to evaluate as you go along so that you can adapt and change as necessary.

Exams – Formal tests given to establish what a child has learnt. Exams are fast becoming a key feature of school life and this can put a great deal of pressure on our children. There are various ways in which you can help your children achieve their best in an exam. Give them plenty of practice before the event, so they feel comfortable with the format of the paper. Offer plenty of advice on how to gain maximum marks and also on how best to use the allotted time. Give them help in structuring their revision, teaching them the best approaches to use (for instance, explaining how mind-maps and memory systems work). In addition, make it clear to your children that exams are not the be-all and end-all of their educational experience. Although gaining good results is important, our key aim as teachers is for our children to actually learn, rather than to give proof of what they have learnt to some outside body.

EiC – Excellence in Cities. A government programme offering support for schools in deprived urban areas, particularly focused on secondary education. See www.standards.dfes.gov.uk/sie/eic/ for more information.

Exclusion – Banning a child from school for a set period of time. Exclusions can be temporary, 'fixed term' affairs (also known as 'suspension'), in which the student will soon return to the classroom; alternatively they can be permanent, at which point you will probably heave a sigh of relief and wave with joy as the object of your daily torment rides off into the sunset.

Exhaustion – The feeling that strikes approximately three weeks before the end of term. Alternatively, the sensation that hits after a week in which someone who should know better has deigned to timetable a parents' evening, a twilight staff meeting and a set of reports.

Extra-curricular activities – Activities that take place outside the normal school day, and which provide 'extras' in addition to the statutory curriculum. The teacher who gets him or herself involved with extra-curricular activities will tend to develop a really good reputation in the school, because of the positive relationships that he or she builds with the children outside of lessons. Extra-curricular activities can also be great fun for both teacher and students. The teacher who participates in extra-curricular work will at first be full of enthusiasm (see above), but eventually may become subject to exhaustion (again, see above).

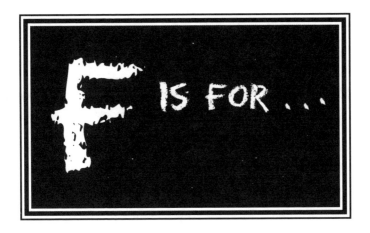

FRUSTRATiONS

Things that disappoint, irritate or annoy us.

There are numerous great things about being a teacher – it's a job with a good portion of fun, enjoyment and pleasure. However, there are also myriad frustrations that plague the hard-working teacher. All of these frustrations have one thing in common: they get in the way of the real job that we all want to do – to teach our classes and help our children learn. I worked in a number of different careers before I became a teacher, and in every job people had some justifiable complaints about their work. However, it does have to be said that as a profession teachers do love a good moan more than most. I guess it's because we do have a lot of things to genuinely get frustrated about, and because doing the job well is so crucial for our children's futures.

The frustrations we experience take place in a number of different settings. First and foremost, they occur inside the classroom, the place where we spend the majority of our time. Here, the silly or aggressive behaviour of a core group of students can be hugely frustrating. Why oh why can't they just behave themselves, we wonder; why do they have to make it so difficult for us to help them to learn?

At the point when these thoughts enter your mind, it's worth taking a moment to remember what it was like to be a school kid. We might want to be there (well, we *might*) but for some children school is a prison full of meaningless hard work that they can hardly wait to escape. And like prisoners on a chaingang, the only way they can hit back is by making life as difficult as possible for their captors. Even for the well motivated, some lessons will seem pointless or boring. So, when this particular frustration hits you hard, take a moment to stand in your children's shoes and see school from their point of view.

Children who talk while I'm trying to teach are a personal bugbear of mine. I'm not asking for anything particularly difficult, so how can it be so hard for them to just be silent and listen for a few minutes? On occasions (some of total desperation), I have turned to myself to try and find fault. Is it that I'm not a good enough teacher to hold their attention? Is it that the work that I'm setting is not challenging/interesting/exciting/well-planned (delete as appropriate) enough? Or could it simply be they have never been taught how to listen to and respect teachers? (When that thought strikes I start to worry about showing my age!)

And how about when you set the work clearly, identifying exactly what you want the students to do, then thirty seconds after the class starts work, five hands go up saying 'what are we meant to do?' I guess this one comes back to listening skills. If they don't bother to or can't listen in the first place, then maybe we need to teach them how to do it? Imagine that – a whole area of the curriculum devoted to learning those really important skills, such as how to listen.

Chasing up kids who don't turn up to detentions is another source of huge irritation, so much so that it can be tempting not to set them in the first place, rather than get involved in an endless game of cat and mouse. The same applies to homework. You set it, in the sure and certain knowledge that you are simply creating a rod for your own back. As you ask for the return of said homework, the naïve hope that you may receive a full set of work flickers temptingly in your heart. Only to be disappointed once again, as three completed homeworks are handed in, along with several scrappy bits of paper on which a maximum of ten words are scrawled.

Taking a moment to look at school from the children's point of view, there are of course plenty of frustrations for them as well. Top of the students' list would probably come the ineffective or ineffectual teacher. If you think back to your own school days, you could probably name a number of teachers who were too strict, too lazy, too weak, too boring. If the teacher cannot control the class, this must be particularly frustrating for the children who want to work, as they are forced to stay in a classroom where nothing is being learnt.

There are lots of environmental frustrations around in schools. Messy classrooms, peeling wallpaper, graffiti, smelly loos, the list is endless. These frustrations impact on the poor kids, as well as on the teachers and other staff. Having worked in some lovely office environments, I know just how important a good working environment is to your enjoyment of your job.

For the secondary school teacher is there anything more conducive to stress than not having your own classroom base? As you rush madly towards the classroom where your next lesson will take place, you hope against hope that you might get there before the children have trashed the room. As you struggle under the load of a huge box containing exercise books, text books and whiteboard pens, several of your students pass by, knocking into you and never even pausing to offer assistance.

I find the whole notion of duty a real frustration. 'Doing my duty' just about sums it up – my duty to who? – it's like a throwback to my days as a girl guide. Let's face it, it's only on the rarest of occasions that a teacher actually manages to take his or her break. Why then compound this misery by snatching away further chunks of time simply for us to stand around in the freezing cold waiting for the bell to summon us back to work? The worst thing about duty is that although other teachers might not turn up to theirs, you just know that if you personally miss so much as thirty seconds of your duty, the duty manager is bound to find out.

The other people that we work with in school can be a source of frustration: teachers who abdicate responsibility for their kids; teachers who don't stick to the agreed procedures of the school; teachers who are lazy or who take sick leave when they don't really need to. Whisper it, in case Chris Woodhead hears, but wouldn't we all admit in private that there are a smallish number of teachers who just can't do the job?

Incompetent managers must come high on this list of 'frustrating other people', although to my mind their idiocy can be pretty amusing on occasions. It's those people who've gone into management not because they want to do it, but because they just can't cut it in the classroom. In the staffroom the frustrations include people moaning and being negative, or those dirty beggars who don't wash up their own cups or who nick your own favourite mug.

Because time is so precious for the hard-pressed teacher, anything that squanders our time will become a source of extreme irritation bordering on anger. For instance those meetings that are a total waste of time – that don't achieve anything except giving the managers a chance to hear the sound of their own voices.

Paperwork is high on many teachers' lists of 'things that p★★s me off'. From the detailed planning that doesn't actually get used in the classroom, to reports that parents don't bother to read. From the meaningless form filling that takes away so much of our valuable time, to those policies created especially for Ofsted inspections, that are instantly relegated to the cupboard the minute the inspectors leave, never to be looked at again.

Above everything else, it's people outside of school who add the most to our frustration quotient. Particular ire must be reserved for the government of the day (it doesn't matter what party). They are the source of those endless new initiatives plucked from the air by people who don't know what they're talking about, which subsequently eat into our valuable time like vicious piranhas. The fact that the government doesn't trust teachers to just get on with the job like competent professionals is a low blow to our morale.

Other top offenders include incompetent LEAs and parents who don't bring up their children properly, but who then expect the teachers to solve everything and somehow manage to educate them as well. Finally, let me name the whole testing caboodle of SATs and league tables as a chief culprit and a source of constant irritation to many. The inherent belief is that if we can't test something, it simply doesn't count. Just consider this: what hope did Van Gogh have of getting an 'A' in GCSE Art? I rest my case.

F is also for . . .

Faculty – A way of grouping related disciplines or subjects together in the secondary school. The alternative to the faculty is the department, generally a smaller grouping of subjects or single subjects. To give one example, a school might have an Art Department, or an Arts Faculty. The former would involve only art teachers, the latter might include art, drama, dance and music teachers.

Fail – Not to succeed at something. Any system that views success as vital will leave little room for the less able. Children who experience constant feelings of failure will tend to become negative about themselves, and what they can achieve. The same applies to schools labelled as 'failing'.

Fair – To treat people in a reasonable and equitable manner. Children view 'being fair' as a key attribute in their teachers. Although there will inevitably be some children that you like more than others (see 'Favourites' below), it is vital to remain fair in your dealings with the class. Being fair means being reasonable – for instance understanding that giving a whole class a detention for the entire morning break is not really on. As well as being unfair on the children, it is also unfair on the teachers who have to work with them later on that day.

Fast track – A scheme whereby teachers are 'fast-tracked' to leadership positions. Applicants can be ITT students or serving teachers.

Favourites – To prefer one person to others, and to treat them better because of this preference. It is only human nature for us to like some of the children we teach more than we like others. However, it is a big mistake to actually show your like or dislike of a child. Students very quickly pick up on a teacher who has 'favourites' and will not be impressed.

Fear – To feel scared. For some children, school can be a fearful place. This feeling of fear might come about because they find the work so hard to do. It might also involve feeling scared of other children, or even of the teachers. Teachers can feel fearful too. For instance, that hollow feeling in the pit of the stomach at the start of term – the fear that you might somehow have 'forgotten' how to teach.

Fidget – To wriggle or move about. Children, particularly the very young, will have a lot of natural energy, and this can often come out in fidgeting (particularly if the lesson is boring or requires high levels of concentration). Right from the start it is worth training your children in non-fidgety behaviour. For instance, crossing their legs and arms while sitting on the carpet; not tipping back on their chairs or tapping pencils while the teacher is talking. It has recently been suggested that the children who fidget most are likely to be kinaesthetic learners. Giving these children a piece of plasticine with which to fiddle can provide a good way to channel their energy.

Fight – A physical attack by one person on another. Having to break up fights is one of the scariest aspects of being a teacher. There seems to be something within human nature that takes pleasure in witnessing a fight. (Think about the huge audiences for boxing matches, or the shouts of 'fight, fight, fight' that urge on an altercation in the playground.) If you are put in a position where you must stop a fight, think first of the safety of the other children and also of yourself. The law allows you to use 'reasonable force' to break up fighting students, but also helpfully states that 'there is no legal definition' of this term. Of course, if you are a witness to two students trying to seriously hurt each other, your natural instinct will be to stop the fight.

File – To put papers away in a particular order. Filing is possibly one of the most boring administrative jobs ever invented. It's one of those jobs that you put aside for a rainy day when you have nothing better to do. Given that there is always something better to do, the pile of papers labelled 'to file' will often gather dust for many years. (Author's note: if something has not been filed for over a year, and you haven't missed it, then why not file it under 'B' for 'bin'?)

Finish – To complete something. Teachers will often use the word 'finish', as in 'Have you finished your work yet?' Unfortunately, there is often a wide gulf between work that a child says is 'finished' and what the teacher believes to be complete.

Flexibility – The ability to bend or adapt to suit differing circumstances. Flexibility is another one of those 'key attributes of the successful teacher'. Although we do need to be completely clear about our expectations, there will be times when we have to relax or bend a little in order to deal best with a situation.

Form tutor – A teacher who has pastoral responsibility for a class in the secondary school. This responsibility includes taking the register, overseeing the students' progress and behaviour in all their subjects, and so on. If you're ever given a choice of which form group you want (OK, I admit it's unlikely), then choose either (a) Year 7, who can be moulded into 'Stepford Students', or (b) Year 11, who disappear from school once external exams start, giving you a well-deserved break.

Funny – To be amusing. The teacher who is able to be funny and see the funny side when things go wrong will create a positive feeling within the classroom, and will develop good relationships with his or her children.

GROUP WORK

A number of people working together.

Group work goes in and out of fashion as an approach for learning. (If I was going to be a bit 'deep' about it, perhaps its popularity is a reflection of the prevailing views in society on the importance of the individual versus the collective.) Sometimes 'whole-class teaching' will be in the ascendancy: the teacher actively teaching or lecturing to the class, and the individual students listening or making notes. At other times the power of learning within a group will be highlighted: the teacher facilitating the work so that the children can learn together. (Of course, most teachers will sensibly make use of a range of approaches, regardless of what is currently viewed as 'best'.)

With group work comes the acceptance that the teacher can let go of the reins once in a while and let the children direct their own learning. The fear of what might happen when we do this (will they stay on task?) means that we might tend to avoid group work and stick to individual activities. This is perhaps particularly so early on in our careers when we are less sure about our classroom management skills.

Group work offers a wide range of benefits, and will assist

your students in mastering lots of important skills. Working within a group means that the children learn from each other, sharing their ideas, abilities and opinions. It is also excellent for developing the skills of cooperation and consideration. The group format asks that the children learn to listen to each other, that they consider what others have to say, and are supportive of other people's ideas and feelings. Working together with others will develop the children's social skills and encourage them to value other people.

The group offers a great forum for the sharing and exchanging of ideas. The children can build an idea together, getting feedback and help from others as they move along. They can look at different opinions or viewpoints, or explore their own and others' knowledge about, or responses to, a topic. To a certain extent, group work also takes the pressure off the teacher for a while, although it does mean being 'hot' on your classroom management.

The groups that you use might range in size from pairs to the whole class working together as a group. Of course, the way in which you use group work will depend on the age of your students and also the subject you are teaching. Some areas of the curriculum do lend themselves more naturally to group work than others, for instance drama and PE are particularly orientated towards the use of groups. However, group work can play a really valuable role in any subject that you care to name.

To organize and work with groups effectively takes a surprisingly high level of classroom management skill. There are plenty of opportunities for disaster along the way, although the more often you set up and use group work, the easier you will find it to manage. The first step is actually getting the children into groups – in fact more difficult than it might sound.

Left to their own devices, your children will happily sort themselves into groups. Unfortunately, the friendship groupings that result may not be particularly conducive to good work and behaviour. When working with friends there is a natural tendency for the children to drift off the task and into social chatter. In addition, you will have the problem of your 'sad Sammys', the lonely or socially inexperienced children with whom no one wants to work. You then have to allocate him/

her to a group and deal with the resulting complaints. There is an additional problem in that kids will either (if young) divide themselves on gender lines, or (if older) divide according to 'gangs' or boy/girlfriends.

You can of course design the make-up of the groups yourself, deciding exactly which combinations will work best. This requires quite a lot of pre-organization and is also dependent on the teacher having a good idea of the children's personalities. In the primary school, where the teacher works closely with one class, he or she will have a good sense of any potential problems with different mixtures of children. For the secondary teacher who knows his or her classes less well, teacher-organized groupings can be a recipe for disaster.

Random groupings work well, particularly for activities where the children will only be working together for a short period of time. Perhaps the easiest way to organize random groups is via a numbering system. Here's how to do it: count how many children there are in the class, then divide this by the number of students you want in each group. Ask the children to count out loud up to this number around the room, with the number they call out denoting their group. For example, if you want to get groups of three in a class of twenty-seven, the children would need to count around the class or circle up to nine. The number ones would then work together, the number twos, and so on. Impressively, some children quickly suss out this numbering method and put themselves into a certain order so that they end up working with their friends. To get over this problem, start the counting from a different point in the class, for instance in the middle of the circle or the room.

When you first begin using group work with a class, it is a good idea to make your expectations and requirements crystal clear. For instance, when working with a new Year 7 class, I introduce boy/girl pairs right from the start. At first the children complain, but they very quickly forget to moan and learn just to get on with it. When working in groups, you will find that the noise levels in your classroom might be quite loud. This means that you must have a signal to indicate that you want the class to quieten down. I use a 'noise-o-meter' graph drawn on the board and ask the children to keep the noise below a certain level.

There will also be times when you want to stop the groups to give an instruction. To make this as simple as possible, and to avoid the need to shout above the racket, you should agree a signal for the groups to stop working and listen to the teacher. This 'pull back' signal might be a hand raised in the air, a sharp noise or some other type of non-verbal command.

One of the most powerful forms of group work is when the whole class works together as a single group. This is hard to set up and manage, but when it falls into place it brings a really magical feeling into the room – a sense that the children are genuinely cooperating and in doing so, creating something really special. I do a number of whole-class group activities in my drama lessons. The simplest of these involves asking the children to walk around the room. They must then, without making any specific signal, all stop at exactly the same moment. Getting this right involves concentration and awareness, plus the ability to work as a single unit.

Another really effective whole-class exercise is the creation of a whole-class soundtrack. This requires the whole class to lie down in a circle on the floor, with their heads just touching ear-to-ear in the centre. I then give the class a setting (the seaside, an asylum, night time in New York) and they must work together to build a soundtrack for this location. The activity is far harder than it sounds – the temptation at first is for everyone to join in simultaneously – resulting in a pointless cacophony of sound. The students soon start to realize that they must listen to the group as a whole, and only contribute when appropriate. When the class finally gets the message, and begins working as one, there is a powerful sense of unity in the room.

G is also for . . .

GTC – The General Teaching Council: a series of regional bodies set up to promote the status of teachers and to ensure high professional standards. Teachers must be registered with the relevant GTC to work in the state education system in the UK. The formation of the GTC has not proved particularly popular with teachers. For more details, see www.gtc.org.uk (England), www.gtcni.org.uk (Northern Ireland), www.gtcs.org.uk (Scotland) and www.gtcw.org.uk (Wales).

Gifted and talented – A term describing those children who have a 'gift' or a 'talent' (i.e. a high level of ability) in a particular subject or subjects. The term divides ability into 'gift' for academic subjects and 'talent' for practical or artistic areas of the curriculum, such as PE or drama. There is a National Academy for gifted and talented youth (see www.warwick.ac.uk/ gifted/ for details). For more information on the area of gifted and talented children, see www.nc.uk.net/gt/index.html.

Gossip – Talking about other people, usually in a negative way. Teachers will of course gossip about each other and their students/classes (although this is usually a moan rather than a gossip). Of course, our students will gossip about us too. A particular favourite for the students is when they realize that two of their teachers might be having a 'thing' together. This kind of gossip can circulate the school for weeks, along the way falling prey to the 'Chinese whisper' syndrome, whereby the names and details get mixed up with occasionally hilarious results.

Some student gossip can be quite hurtful, but the teacher who gets wound up by it will only give them an incentive to gossip even more. Better to brush it off or perhaps use it to help develop your personal teacher 'mystique'. I was once spotted by a student putting an arm around another female teacher (us drama types are quite touchy-feely). The student came up to me the next day and asked 'Miss, are you a lesbian?'. My deadpan response of 'Why, do you fancy me?' left her speechless.

Governors – The members of a 'governing body' set up to oversee the running of a school. School governors are volunteers drawn from all different sectors – parents, staff, the LEA, the community. For more information, see www.governornet. co.uk or www.governyourschool.co.uk.

GTP – The Graduate Teacher Programme, part of the GRTP (Graduate and Registered Teacher Programme). Teachers doing the GTP will work within a school to gain qualified teacher status, being paid a salary and being given training and support while they work. Competition for places is hot. For more information, see www.tta.gov.uk/php/read.php?sectionid=30.

HOMEWORK

School work that is done at home.

In theory (and in the dreams of PGCE tutors, parents, head teachers and Ofsted inspectors), homework consists of activities carefully planned by the teacher as a preparation for, or an extension of, learning done in the classroom. In this theoretical dream world, the children make a careful note of exactly what they must do for homework, planning out each evening's working time so that everything is completed to perfection. In the home, there is plenty of space for the child to do the work, and the television is turned off during the time that the homework is being done.

On the day that the piece is due (we're still in our dream world here), the children remember to bring their homework into school, lovingly packing it in their bags. At the relevant moment every child in the class presents his or her work to the teacher — complete and beautifully presented. 'I learnt so much from doing that, miss,' the child says, 'I'm really looking forward to seeing what you think about it.' The teacher subsequently spends hours marking the work, and then returns it to each child, with detailed comments, in the following lesson. Well, that's the theory.

Let's take a reality check now and see what might actually happen during the life of an average piece of homework. First of all, the 'carefully planned' part of the equation is a little bit hit and miss. On occasions, (how numerous these are will depend on the individual teacher) the work is decided in his or her head approximately two seconds before it is actually set. It will probably have some vague connection to the work currently going on in the classroom. Some of the children might scribble down a quick note about what the teacher has asked them to do. Others will trust to memory (or to a 'keeno' class mate to remind them nearer the time).

On arriving at home, some of the more motivated students will put aside the half hour between dinner and the start of *Eastenders* to complete all the homework that has been set that day. (This assumes that the child has somewhere to actually do the work – for many this is a real problem.) Others will have a more relaxed view of the term 'home' work, preferring instead to complete the piece in the playground/toilets/corridor five minutes before the lesson. About half of those who have taken the trouble to take the term literally and actually do the work at home will have forgotten to pack it in their bags.

When the teacher asks for the return of said homework, a scrabble will ensue in which five scrappy pieces of paper are actually handed in. The rest will have fallen prey to the usual array of excuses: dogs that enjoy nothing better than a diet of homework papers apparently being the main culprit. At this point the exhausted teacher heaves a sigh of relief because he or she only has five short bits of work to actually mark.

There are various approaches that you can take to overcome all the problems that I've listed above. You might decide to reward those who do their homework properly and hand it in on time. You could also sanction any students who fail to complete the task, although this can turn into an administrative nightmare as you chase the children to actually serve the punishment. A more positive idea is to re-think the types of homework that you actually set in the first place. Rather than always giving written work, with all the attendant problems, you might on occasions think laterally about what can be done at home.

You could set the children a poem to memorize, a book to read, some research to do. You might ask them to interview their friends and family for a project, or to find resources for the next lesson. When writing is required, why not give the class a long-term project so that you can set 'work on your project' as a homework for a number of lessons? Although there will be children who fail to do any work on the project until the day before it is due, you can at least conveniently 'overlook' this fact.

Finally, do take the trouble to look at homework from your children's perspective. If it sometimes seems to us that we're setting homework because we have to, rather than because we believe in its true worth, then this message will inevitably filter through to our children. At secondary level, the students will be receiving work from various different teachers, and this can lead to a heavy workload that piles on the stress for the more conscientious students.

H is also for . . .

Head of department – The person in charge of a department of teachers in the secondary school.

Head teacher – The person in charge of running a school. I've encountered a wide variety of head teachers during the course of my career in education (some good, some rather less so). Generally speaking, there are three different types of head. Type 'A' takes a 'hands off' approach, staying in the office and employing strong deputies to do the legwork. This type of head is interested in the managerial and financial aspects of school life, and is unlikely to sully his or her hands by actually teaching.

Type 'B' is a 'figurehead' for the school, and will sometimes use the title head master or mistress. This type uses a 'strict and scary' style of management, in which no one is allowed to use his or her first name (not even the teachers). The 'figurehead' will often be seen striding the corridors looking terrifying, the students parting like the Red Sea at his approach. This head might teach one or two lessons a week, but most likely in traditional subjects such as Latin.

Finally, type 'C' uses a 'hands on' approach to the job of being a head. He or she still has one foot in the classroom, and is keen to get to know both the children and the staff. The 'hands on' head builds positive relationships with everyone at the school, and makes good use of incentives to encourage both students and teachers.

Hell – The biblical location of the Devil, opposite to Heaven. Can also be used to mean horrible, difficult, nasty, as in 'the class from hell'.

Holidays – Time off from work, or to travel away from home. Next time you're tempted to complain about having to work during your holidays, take a moment to consider the holiday entitlement of the 'average Joe'. I used to work in an office before I became a teacher, and we would get around twenty days' holiday a year.

Humour – Funny, causing people to laugh, or being able to see the funny side of things. As in the dating ads, having a good sense of humour (or 'GSOH') is absolutely essential if you want to be a teacher, especially if you plan to stay in the profession for the long term. You'll need to be able to laugh in so many situations: from the willingness to incorporate humour into your classroom to the ability to get amused when the latest government initiative arrives.

IMAGINATION

The ability to 'see' and believe in things that don't really exist.

Children find it very easy to inhabit the world of the imagination: in fact they can sometimes find it difficult to work out where reality ends and imagination begins. Imagination can help children to explore and deal with their fears. Some figments of the imagination can be quite scary, for instance a fear of the monster under the bed. Imagination can also help us to 'experience' things beyond the limits of our normal world. A young child playing with water and sand might imagine that her boat is sailing across the sea to a magical land. A group of children playing with dolls in the dressing up corner could be creating a pretend family of their own.

As we grow older, we start to feel a bit silly or embarrassed by our imaginations. Although our children usually start school with their imaginations intact, the education system soon beats it out of them. Where the focus is on learning skills and practising techniques, there is little space for imaginative play beyond the early years setting.

There are lots of ways in which you can use the imagination in your teaching. Not only does this increase the children's engagement with the work, but it also makes your job a lot more fun. Asking the children to 'be' something or someone else is a very powerful classroom technique, and is a great way of making school seem more relevant to normal, everyday life. Our students love to take on a fictional role, and they will often approach the work with great seriousness. For instance, you could ask the children to take on the role of football managers, creating their own team, designing a kit and a new stadium, and devising and writing a football programme.

I was once told a story which illustrates the power of imagination (both that of the teacher and that of the children). The story was about a teacher who, last lesson every Friday, would take her class on a magical journey into the imagination. She would spread out a big Persian rug in her classroom, which became a 'magic carpet' for the duration of the lesson. The whole class would squeeze onto the rug for the trip. If they were going somewhere cold, the teacher would ask the children to take off their blazers, then she would open all the windows and turn on a big fan. On the other hand, if they were going somewhere hot, the teacher would get them to put on lots of layers, close all the windows tight, and make them sweat it out.

You can actually take a journey into the imagination without any props at all. Ask your children to close their eyes and imagine themselves to be somewhere different, then talk to them about what they see, allowing space for them to invent the details. For a relaxing journey, you might suggest a beach on a Caribbean island, talking about all the beautiful sensations – the hot sun, the warm sand, the cool sea, the breeze in the palm trees. For a more exciting trip, you could drop them off into a deep dark forest, where hidden dangers lurk.

A quick word of warning about using imaginative activities in your classroom – sometimes the children will take you very literally and you will need to point out that the work is a fiction. For instance, I often use a scenario where I set up a crime scene in my room and get the class to play the role of police detectives who must solve the crime. I start the lesson by telling the children that there has been a murder. At this point, depending on the age of the children, I am sometimes asked 'What really, miss!?' If I'm working with very young students, it's important to step out of the fiction for a moment to tell them that this is only a story. Although it might be tempting to laugh at the more sensitive children for being 'gullible', this response is in fact a perfect illustration of how powerful our imaginations can be.

I is also for . . .

Improvement – Getting better at something. The term 'improving school' is a wonderful euphemism for a school which is getting better, but which hasn't quite made it yet.

Improvisation – Making it up as you go along. Although technically speaking 'improvisation' is a term from the drama lesson, in fact all good teachers are great at improvising. With the teacher taking the role of principal actor in the classroom, he or she will have to improvise a way through a range of potential scenarios.

Inclusion – A policy whereby children with special educational needs are 'included' in mainstream education. The policy of inclusion is a great idea in theory, but the practice often leaves something to be desired. (See 'Behaviour' for more thoughts on the subject of inclusion.)

Independent school – Another name for a private school, one which is 'independent' from the state system.

IEP – Individual Education Plan. A plan tailored to an individual child with special educational needs. The IEP outlines targets, teaching strategies and provision for a child with SEN.

Induction – A programme of entry into teaching, taken by newly qualified teachers. Teachers who pass their induction year will achieve qualified teacher status, or QTS. For more information and thoughts about induction, see 'NQT'.

ICT – Information and Communication Technology. A school subject dealing with computers and other related technologies.

Teachers are increasingly expected to use ICT in their own teaching, and to have a good level of knowledge and skill in this area.

ITT – Initial Teacher Training. The name given to courses for students training to become teachers.

INSET – In-Service Education and Training. Training for teachers who are already working in a school. INSET is also known as 'continuing professional development', or CPD. If you go out of school on some INSET, you'll have a great day, a fantastic lunch and you might just learn something new. Bear in mind, though, that on your return your classroom will probably look as though it has been hit by a bomb.

Inspire – To give someone the feeling that they want to and can do something. The very best teachers have the ability to inspire their children. One of the reasons I went into teaching was because of a handful of inspirational teachers that I myself had as a child. The same probably applies to many who have come into the profession.

Intake – The body of children coming into a school. The type of intake that a school has will inevitably have an impact on how 'well' it does.

Interactive whiteboard – A computerised whiteboard which allows the teacher and students to 'interact' with what is on the screen. Children can make marks or write on the board, teachers can have a variety of windows open, or show colourful Powerpoint presentations.

Internet – A system of linked computers around the world, which allows people to share information and to communicate with each other. The wonderful world of the web provides teachers and students with access to vast quantities of in-formation. The problem is sifting through everything on offer to establish what is actually going to be of use. Although a valuable tool in lessons, using the internet can bring with it a

great deal of stress. The difficulties include problems with
access, web pages that go missing, children going into chat
rooms when they should be working, or the downloading of
inappropriate material. The teacher must also be aware of the
issue of safety when using the internet. For an interesting
overview of net safety, and some useful links, see
www.philb.com/childsafe.htm.

Invigilation – Overseeing children who are taking an examination. Invigilation is possibly one of the most boring jobs that
has ever been known to humankind. In theory, the 'Workload
Agreement' should mean that teachers will no longer be
required to invigilate external examinations. For those who have
never experienced the 'pleasures' of invigilation, the mind-
numbing tedium of pacing up and down an examination room
while handing out the occasional sheet of paper is hard to
describe. However, being resourceful individuals, teachers have
of course come up with plenty of ways to pass the time. A few
from my own experience are, worryingly, actually too 'naughty'
to print. However, for an amusing account of the printable
'exam hall games' which teachers devise, you might like to look
at news.bbc.co.uk/1/hi/education/3742915.stm.

JOB INTERVIEWS

A meeting at which you are tested to check your suitability for a job.

Teaching interviews really are a very curious thing, designed to suit the employer (the school) rather than the prospective employee (that's you). If you've never worked outside of the world of teaching, then perhaps the interview system doesn't seem all that strange. However, if you have come into teaching after working in another career, then you will probably find the teaching interview a totally bizarre experience.

For a start, actually getting to the stage of being offered an interview can take up huge quantities of potentially wasted time. Filling in the endless pages of those LEA application forms should, it strikes me, be seen as sufficient evidence of your enthusiasm and commitment. Then there's the 'letter of application' – a detailed summary of all your attributes and how they suit you for this particular post. It's a good idea to have a standard letter of application on a computer, which you can tailor to suit the individual job. Amazingly, considering the focus on ICT in education, there will still be some schools who insist on a handwritten letter of application. In these circumstances you will inevitably have reached the final sentence of your two page missive when you make a spelling mistake. ('Never use tippex', the advice manuals advise.)

Once you are over that hurdle and by some miracle (considering all that tippex) you are actually invited to an interview, things take a turn for the worse. Rather than simply facing an hour or so of questions at a time fixed to suit your circumstances, a typical teaching interview will eat up all or much of a whole day. All the candidates will be present at the school at one time, leading to the strange situation where you can end up becoming quite friendly with those against whom you are competing for the job.

You will be taken on a 'tour' of the school, designed to show you only what the school deems desirable. This means a visit to beautifully behaved classes and top class facilities (which may prove to be rather a fictional version of the school if you actually get the job). At the end of a long day, you will be asked to make an instant decision about whether or not to take the job, based on these fleeting impressions of what the working environment will actually be like.

There are various ways that you can improve your chances of success at an interview. You might feel that it is best to portray the 'real you'. However, it is important to accept that you are playing a game, and those who play best are most likely to win the prize of a job. For a start, do go dressed for the occasion, and to suit the job for which you are applying. At secondary level, if you are hoping to teach a 'creative' subject such as art or drama, then a little bit of flair in the clothes you choose will probably be acceptable. In all other instances, you would be advised to play it safe, and to choose a smart but comfortable 'business suit' style atire. For the primary school, do wear smart clothes, but make sure that you would actually be able to teach in them. A short skirt and high heels are absolutely no use at all when it comes to kneeling on the carpet beside a five-year-old.

During the formal interview, make eye contact with the person asking you a question, and try not to fidget in your seat. It might sound obvious, but it is important to show that you like children. Give examples from your own experience to illustrate any points that you make. Even as a student teacher, you will have examples from your teaching practice that you can bring into the discussion.

It has always struck me as strange that teachers are not always made to demonstrate their ability to actually teach. If the school does ask you to teach a sample lesson, then the following advice might be of help. Don't plan to do too much – having a clearly structured start and finish to the lesson will score you points on classroom management. Don't worry too much about difficult behaviour – with the head or another senior teacher watching it is unlikely that the children will try it on. Aim to utilize a range of different teaching approaches, using some of your favourite tried and tested lesson ideas (this is not the time to experiment).

If you are offered the job, there are various indicators that will give you some idea about whether the school will be a positive place at which to work. Happy, smiling children are a key factor – if you get the chance, check out the atmosphere around the school at break times and, at secondary level, between lessons. Look around you at the environment itself – colourful displays and a lack of graffiti are good signs. If you do get the chance, try to sideline one of the teachers currently working at the school for a quiet chat.

If you're a mature student going into your NQT year, and you feel that you deserve extra pay for your experience outside of school, then the interview is the time to establish your salary expectations. A promise made at this point is more likely to be followed through. Finally, if you do fail to get the job, then I guess you'll just have to console yourself with the usual advice to 'put it down to experience'.

J is also for...

January – The first month of the calendar year. January can be a very tough time to be a teacher. You arrive at and leave school in the dark. The fun days of Christmas are long behind; the halcyon days of summer are a long way ahead. If getting through the school year was like climbing a mountain range, January would be like standing deep in a valley and looking up at the highest peak. It sure is a long way to climb to make it to July.

Jargon – Terminology used by people within a specific area of work. Teaching is full of jargon. These technical sounding terms serve to distance us from normal people and make us sound like we know what we're doing.

Joke – Telling a funny tale. Teachers who have a good repertoire of jokes are always popular with children. I can still remember my history teacher at junior school. He would bounce into the classroom, leap onto a desk and tell us dirty jokes about characters from history. He certainly got our attention.

KEYS

Small metal items used to unlock doors.

Like something out of *Prisoner: Cell Block H*, teachers can often be seen wandering the corridors of the school jangling their keys. Unfortunately, theft is a part of life in schools these days. Sometimes it's the students themselves who can't be trusted; sometimes the threat comes from burglars in the local area. I'm sure there are some schools out there in which things that are not locked away do not disappear. However, it really is worth getting into the habit of locking your valuables away (even during lessons where I once caught a kid rifling through my handbag).

While on the subject of keys, do make sure that you don't leave them in the door of the room while you're inside it and any children are outside. On a recent training course, a teacher told me the story of the time she got locked in the stock cupboard. She had left the keys in the door, and children being children they had decided to lock her in. It was hours before a passing teacher heard her cries.

Of course, one of the problems inherent in everything being locked away is the danger of the missing bunch of keys. In one school where I taught, the loss by a deputy of his set of keys had wide scale repercussions. Unfortunately this particular set of keys was a 'full set', including ones that opened the computer rooms, the finance office, and the school safe containing a priceless set of silver trophies (OK, I made that last bit up). Convinced that the keys had been stolen by a student, there was no alternative but to change all the locks. The expense was swallowed with poor grace by the head teacher. The shame-faced deputy later admitted to some of the staff (in private, well out of the head teacher's hearing) that he'd found the keys at home that night.

K is also for . . .

Keeno – Slang term used to describe a child who works hard at school. The kids with a reputation to uphold will take special pleasure in winding up the keenos for being 'Miss's pet'. See also 'Boffin'.

Kids – Affectionate term for children. Although formally called pupils, students or children, I still find it hard not to think of every child I've ever taught as one of my 'kids'.

Knackered – Exhausted, completely worn out. The feeling that strikes most teachers as the end of term draws near.

LESSON PLANS

An outline of a lesson, giving details of the learning that is going to take place.

When you're a student teacher, lesson plans are typically a three page affair, beautifully presented, full of detail and ICT-ed to within an inch of their lives. Your masterpiece will give a detailed breakdown of your 'starter', 'development' and 'plenary' activities, proposed timings for every section of the lesson, information about any children with special needs, ideas for differentiation, and so on and on and on.

By the time you've been teaching for a few years, you might have resorted to scribbling down a few ideas on the back of a fag packet five minutes before you enter the classroom. You could be reusing scraps of paper with scribbled notes from the previous year's lessons. You might take a passing glance at a beautiful and detailed scheme of work created as part of your departmental development plan. Or even (dare I say it?) you might on occasions teach without using a lesson plan at all.

Of course, when Ofsted appear, those experienced teachers who have managed perfectly well without actually writing everything down in triplicate will suddenly and magically revisit the skill of writing lesson plans.

Writing detailed plans does of course have its benefits. Clearly, a well-planned lesson is reasonably likely to be a good one. Obviously, we want to factor in differentiated tasks if we possibly can, planning for extension activities or for children with learning difficulties.

Knowing exactly what we're going to teach also allows us to give the children an overview of the lesson before we start – a kind of 'map' of the lesson journey. We can tell them what we're planning to cover, what they might learn from it, and the different types of activities that they're going to do. However, it does strike me that prescriptive planning sometimes goes against the nature of what teaching should be. In many ways, giving a lesson is like giving a performance.

There are some situations where you'll be in the middle of a lesson and things will start to go pear shaped. Perhaps the kids aren't responding as you thought they would, maybe the work is obviously too hard for their level of ability. In these situations, the best teachers have the confidence and flexibility to throw the lesson plan away. (Although perhaps a more interesting approach would be to make a paper aeroplane out of it and get the class to watch you launch it from the window!)

The 'powers that be' would love us to plan every single lesson in detail: the 'this is what you must teach and this is how you must teach it' approach of all those national strategies. It seems that they don't trust that we might be able to improvise on occasions, that they don't believe we can respond to our children's learning on a minute by minute basis, that they don't want us to follow a good lead when the children offer it to us. Having a detailed written plan also gives the critical observer something to 'test' us against. Have we achieved those detailed 'learning objectives', did we get the timing of the lesson right? (This reminds me of a conference at which I once spoke, where I was told that a green card would be held up when I had twenty minutes left, then an orange one for ten minutes, and a red one when I was to stop. I had to laugh at the assumption that I would be watching to see the cards, rather than taking the trouble to use my watch.)

It's my belief that there are various problems inherent in using a really detailed plan for every single one of your lessons.

For a start, too much reliance on what you've written down can lead to a really stilted delivery, particularly where detailed timings are included. I saw a lesson plan once, and I kid you not, that detailed what would happen down to the nearest minute. 9.03am – explain aims of lesson, 9.07am – hand out exercise books. (I was tempted to graffiti on the plan: 9.09am – try to quell riot as children rebel against clock-watching teacher.) In any case, getting the timing right will be an issue at the start of your career: I still try to fit too much into my lessons and I'm an experienced teacher.

In addition to this stilted feeling, when you include a lot of detail it can be tempting to stick to what you've planned, even if it isn't working as you thought it would. Before the event, it really is hard to anticipate how your children will respond and react to a lesson, and whether it will suit their needs. This is especially so if you lack experience because you simply won't have had a chance to try out a variety of things. I still have a vivid memory of trying to teach geography to a class of five-year-olds. I had planned (in minute detail) a lesson using a globe. It very quickly dawned on me that the children barely know where the local shops were.

The other issue that bugs me about detailed lesson planning is that it automatically assumes that the teacher will decide on exactly what should happen in the lesson. Excuse me, but doesn't that rather leave the children out of the equation? Here's a question for you. You're a primary school teacher and you have just launched into your carefully planned lesson when a child pulls a small container out of his pocket. In it is a rare and beautiful stag beetle. 'I just found this in the playground, sir, and I didn't want it to get trodden on so I rescued it,' he says. 'Do you think we should go and release it into the nature area?' It's a lovely sunny day outside. Do you (a) go 'oh that's nice, now give it to sir and let's get on with the lesson', before returning to your master plan (it's 9.03am after all, and you're meant to be explaining your aims), or do you (b) veer off into an impromptu science lesson, heading outside into the sunshine and sitting the children on the grass to look at and draw the beetle, before releasing it back into the wild?

When it comes to what works best, I can only really

comment from my own teaching experience. This experience confirms for me that some of my very best lessons are those for which I did the least planning. Where I had an idea or two in my head, or a couple of key resources, and simply went into the classroom and 'winged' it. Teaching like that is real 'seat of the pants' stuff, but it's fun, you feel like you're alive, and it means you're responding to the reality of the kids in front of you, rather than how you had hoped they would react.

If you're reading this as a student teacher, please accept that you will have to write detailed lesson plans to pass your course. If you're an NQT, and your school has provided you with a set of schemes of work and lesson plans to follow, then please use this – it will save you time and give you a solid foundation from which to start. However, if anyone 'up high' is reading this, please please stop expecting every single detail of every single lesson to be written down. Learning can be a fluid as well as a structured process: sometimes it will be best to let the children take us by the hand and decide on the direction of their own learning.

L is also for . . .

Lateral thinking – Thinking that takes you sideways from the original starting point. Making lateral jumps and connections within a topic is a complex thinking process. It is an important skill in developing creativity and creative thinking. The originator of the term was Edward de Bono.

League table – A table showing the relative success of schools in an area, based mainly on their examination results. This term used to be linked to the placing of football teams within a league system, but is now inextricably connected to school performance. If your school is at the top of the table, then league tables might seem like a great idea. But if your school is right down the bottom, then the publication of a league table showing this can be a source of despair. Putting anything into a league means that someone will come at the top and someone at the bottom. This is all very well in the commercial world, but teaching is about the kids, and no child is going to feel good about seeing their school 'failing' in relation to others. Although league tables now identify the 'value' added by a school, there are many external factors that can impact on the results. To search for league tables by school or area, see www.dfes.gov.uk/performancetables/.

Learning styles – The way in which we learn. There has been much focus recently on the different learning styles of individual children. The three main styles are visual, auditory and kinaesthetic (abbreviated to the acronym 'VAK'), with a fourth, 'tactile' style sometimes used in addition. The idea is that teachers find ways to suit their teaching to the individual styles of each learner (see 'Differentiation' for some more thoughts on this subject).

LSA – Learning Support Assistant. A person who supports learning in the classroom. The LSA typically works with individuals who have special educational needs.

Letter of application – A letter outlining your talents and achievements, written when applying for jobs. An effective letter of application will be tailored to meet the requirements outlined in the job advertisement. Although it is inadvisable to tell any downright fibs, it is usually possible to mould your experience to fit what the school will want to hear.

Library – A place from which books are loaned out. The school library is also sometimes known as the 'Learning Resource Centre'. In the tougher schools, the bookish and the boffins often use the library as a place of refuge from their more free-spirited counterparts.

Literacy – A skel wot hour childrun r sposed two hav bfour thay leaf skool.

Literacy hour – An hour of literacy teaching used in primary schools, which forms part of the 'Literacy Strategy'. The hour must be divided up into three sections: a 'starter' (i.e. the introduction), a 'development' (i.e. the middle bit) and a 'plenary' (i.e. a review of what's been learned). Now who would have thought of dividing lessons in that way if someone hadn't told us? Certainly not experienced teachers with years of expertise, that's for sure.

Literacy Strategy – A government strategy designed to improve literacy. The strategy outlines the terms and techniques that must be taught at the various stages in a child's education. Some teachers feel that it is overly prescriptive and leaves little room for more creative endeavours. For more information, see www.standards.dfes.gov.uk/literacy/.

LEA – Local Education Authority. The department in a local council that deals with education in the area. Some LEAs are innovative, supportive, forward thinking organizations, some are not.

MARKING

Making an assessment of a child's work by the addition of notations, symbols and written comments.

Marking is yet another of those aspects of teaching where the theory of what should happen outstrips the reality of what actually goes on. In theory, marking should be helpful for our children's learning, a continuous dialogue between child and teacher in which mistakes are corrected and development of the work is encouraged. In reality, marking is often a matter of 'getting it done', of ensuring that a set of papers or exercise books look marked by applying only a series of ticks or crosses. This need to get books 'looking' marked is often a result of pressure from outside the classroom – parents, head teachers or inspectors who want to see it done, rather than as a result of what will actually work best for the children.

Just as with all aspects of the job of a teacher, marking is a balancing act between helping your children learn and having some kind of life for yourself. Unless you are planning to spend every spare minute with a red pen in your hand, you are going to have to make some decisions about what can be marked in detail.

My mum was a teacher, and as a young child I used to beg

her for the chance to mark an exercise book. Through my immature eyes, the application of ticks and crosses to a page seemed like some form of adult magic. If only I'd known at the time how, in later years, I would have loved to have someone do the same for me!

At times marking can be a depressing process, because you see exactly how little the children have listened to or followed your instructions. Lesson after lesson you ask for a title and date at the top of the work, neatly underlined, with the work written in full sentences. No matter how much marking and correction you do, it often seems not to make a blind bit of difference.

When it comes to doing marking, it pays to take time to consider your own motivation and approaches to the task. Do you tend to 'tick and flick'? If you do, the books might look marked, but no real learning is going to take place. Do you prefer to spend time making detailed comments, and do your students actually read and take notice of these? If they don't, then there is little additional value for all that extra time that you've put in. (A good tip is to provide some specific time at the start of the lesson, or when the work is returned, for them to read your comments.)

There are various ways in which you can make the marking you do more effective in improving your children's learning, and also less time consuming for yourself. For a start, do make use of an agreed set of symbols to mark your children's work, to include areas where mistakes are typically made. This might include a '/' to indicate where a new paragraph should come or a '?' to say 'I don't understand what you mean'. Having such a list gives you a kind of 'shorthand' for your marking, and will help speed up the process immeasurably. A list of these symbols should be stuck in the front of the exercise books, where the children can easily refer to it.

Don't always see marking as something that you do for your students. A great deal of learning will take place if the children are asked to mark each other's work. Any piece of work that has only one set of correct answers, such as a spelling test, offers the teacher an opportunity to pass the marking buck. With more complex pieces you might circulate the work around the class, asking the children to give comments in various categories that you define. This gives your students a chance to see other people's ideas, and also for the less well-motivated to see what can be achieved with a bit of hard work.

Another great tip is to mark for a specific error, advising your children beforehand that this is what you are going to do. So it is that one day you might ask the class to focus on correct punctuation, another day you might look in detail at spelling, on another occasion you could look to see whether the content of the work is of a high quality. Of course, there will always be those accusations that 'teachers don't bother to correct spelling mistakes anymore'. Always remember that learning is more than just correct technique, and don't let yourself be forced into simply ticking another box.

Above all else, the key thing to bear in mind with marking is to make it actually work for you and for your children. It might sound hopelessly radical, but you could even have a chat with them about what they think would be the best approach.

M is also for ...

Management – Those members of staff who have taken on extra managerial responsibilities outside the classroom. There are various different motivations for becoming a member of the management of a school, particularly when it comes to senior management. One of the best motivations will be the desire to have a say in the overall running of a school and to genuinely 'make a difference' for the children. (I suspect that this is the initial motivation for many.) However, other less noble motivations will also come into play. Of course, the wish to earn a bit more money is understandable. However, for some managers there will also be an element of going on a personal power trip.

It has to be said that teachers do not always make good managers. The subject specialist who loves his or her subject and who becomes a head of department might not actually be all that good at managing people and budgets, or doing administration. Whether or not you actually like your managers will be a separate issue from whether you respect them and feel that they do a good job. I have worked under several managers who I believed to be lovely people, but who just couldn't cut it when it came to the promoted role. Similarly, I have worked for a number of managers who I disliked on a personal level, but who did an excellent job of running a school. (In fact, it can actually be quite a good form of stress relief for the staff to moan about these managers behind their backs.) Of course the worst thing of all are those 'David Brent' style managers who want to be liked by their staff, so much so that they try to get you onside at all times by behaving in the most embarrassing way.

Meetings – A gathering of people for the purpose of discussion, decision, etc. When it comes to the value of a meeting, much will depend on whether you are running it or merely attending it. On the one hand, meetings can be the most wonderful, relevant creation ever, where you get to spout endless rubbish to the assembled group of teachers. Alternatively they can be one of the most mind-numbingly boring things you'll ever do in your teaching career (outdone only by invigilation). A useful tip is to sit at the back of the room with a pile of exercise books, and subtly combine 'M' for 'Meeting' with 'M' for 'Marking'.

Mind-mapping – The creation of detailed brainstorm style plans to 'map' the contents of the mind, making use of colour, shapes, images, and so on. This incredibly useful technique was originally developed by Tony Buzan. See www.mind-map. com and www.mind-mapping.co.uk for more details about mind-mapping.

Mobile phone – A phone that can be used without a landline. An ever shrinking technological object, banned from many schools, yet found in 99.9 per cent of schoolchildren's bags.

NQT

Newly qualified teacher – a teacher in his or her first year in the profession.

The first year in any teacher's career is a difficult yet exciting time. You walk into the classroom full of hope, enthusiasm and good ideas, finally feeling that you are a 'proper' teacher. This first year is a time when you are sowing the seeds of your own personal teaching style and beliefs. Although you will have watched the way that others run their classrooms during your teaching degree, it's not until you become a real teacher with your own class or classes that you can work out how you yourself are going to do it.

There are plenty of mistakes that can (and indeed *should*) be made in your NQT year. So much of what I now know about teaching came from making a mess of things in my first year on the job. Getting it wrong is a great way of finding the strategies that you need to use to get it right. Bear in mind that the work of 'becoming' a teacher is never finished, even when your NQT year is over. True teachers always retain a sense of humility about what they still have left to learn.

In some parts of the country, the first year is known as probation. This term rather suggests a bunch of delinquent new teachers who must be watched for crimes against education from dawn to dusk. In other regions, the word 'induction' hints at a secret society of teachers, into which the inexperienced must enter. Although there is a lot of stress put on 'passing' that all-important first year, in reality newly qualified teachers would be better advised to focus on just doing the job to the best of their ability.

In our first year of teaching we are swept along by vast quantities of energy and enthusiasm. Depending on the school at which the NQT works, you may find senior staff (who should know better) taking advantages of these qualities. How, then, do you go about surviving that first year as a teacher? When it comes to the school and the people who are supposed to help you out, what you really need to thrive is good support, a fair balance of children or classes, plus plenty of advice and help when times get tough.

There are countless books on the subject that will give you detailed advice about getting through your NQT year. The only problem is, the last thing you have to spare in your first year is the time needed to read them all. So, if I had to boil my advice down to five key suggestions, these would be:

1. **Pace yourself:** Although enthusiasm is only natural (and to be commended) do make sure that you don't try to do too much – the job will expand or contract to take up the amount of time you are willing to devote to it. If you run yourself into the ground you will not be able to succeed in the classroom. Learn not to take on too much beyond your responsibilities to the children. Bear in mind that the school year is a long one, so don't use all your energy up in the first few weeks or months.

2. **Don't be a perfectionist:** In a job with no real bounds, you have simply got to let some things slide. Learn to know when good enough is good enough. When things go wrong learn to keep a sense of perspective – how much does it really matter if a couple of your lessons are a complete disaster? As I said above, it's making mistakes that really takes your learning forwards.

3. **Be flexible:** Although there is plenty of great advice out there for new teachers, don't feel that you have to follow it to the letter. There are many variables in teaching – different children, different schools, different teacher personalities and styles. Everything you are told needs to be adapted to suit your own personal situation. Be flexible in your teaching as well – the first year is a good time to take some risks, to experiment with some unusual ideas, to try things out and make those all-important mistakes.

4. **Get plenty of support:** Support is absolutely vital for the hard-pressed teacher, whether this is first and foremost from your induction tutor (as it should be), or just from other members of staff. Teachers (and in fact all school staff) are generally great at supporting each other, so take full advantage of every offer of help you are given.

5. **Have fun:** Whenever possible, approach the job with a sense of fun and enjoyment. Learn to laugh with your kids and try out some fun or imaginative lessons. Remember to enjoy yourself outside of school as well, finding ways to let off steam after the working day is done.

N is also for ...

National Curriculum – A government framework giving statutory guidelines covering the content of the curriculum. For more details see: www.nc.uk.net (England), www.ccea.org.uk (Northern Ireland), www.ltscotland. org.uk (Scotland) and www.accac.org.uk/publications/ncorders.html (Wales).

Nits – The name for the eggs laid by head lice, small insects which live on the human scalp. Rather delightfully, the lice feed by sucking blood from your head. Nits are a particular concern in the primary school, where the close proximity to large numbers of children means that infections can spread quickly. Oh the joys of being a teacher!

Numeracy – Having a good basic knowledge of maths. See www.standards.dfes.gov.uk/numeracy/ for more details of the 'Numeracy Strategy'.

O IS FOR . . .

OFSTED

The Office for Standards in Education – the government body responsible for inspecting schools.

The fatal words 'we're having an Ofsted inspection' are enough to strike terror into the heart of even the most fearless teacher. We can cope with little Freddie swearing repeatedly, we can handle little Tania and her constant mood swings, but the thought of having someone else judge our teaching on the basis of what might be a single visit to our classroom seems almost too much to bear. It does sometimes strike me as strange that, as people who spend a good part of our working lives handing out tests to the children, we seem remarkably loathe to be tested ourselves. This is probably because the set up of the whole system seems so unfair.

Ofsted can be the cause of a great deal of stress. Although the week of inspection will obviously be a difficult time, in fact much of the pressure comes in the build-up to an inspection. The current system of giving advance warning means there is plenty of time for the school to get psyched up. The first step is, obviously, to ensure that the school will appear to be nothing like it is in reality. As with a royal visit, there must be no sign of dissent or disarray, no opportunity for rebellion or riot. So it is that displays get pasted on every available surface, the teachers find themselves using up endless trees in a quest to get every-thing written down, and schools might even sneakily exclude the really difficult kids (or send them on a contrived 'work experience' week). Some schools will even get in a company to pre-inspect the place, piling on the pressure before the inspection has even started.

The latest idea of short inspections with very little notice has both its supporters and detractors. I'd like to make an altern-ative and perhaps even more controversial suggestion. How about making inspections literally a 'turn up on the day' affair, where someone knocks at the school door completely unan-nounced to see what is going on. This approach would mean throwing away those rose-tinted glasses through which so many people want to view our schools. It would require an accept-ance of what honestly goes on in schools, on a day-to-day basis.

Yes, teachers do sometimes go into lessons without preparing properly; yes, exercise books do sometimes go unmarked for weeks on end; yes, some children's behaviour is absolutely horrific and some classes are completely out of control. If this is too unpalatable for those that want to inspect us then they need to get down off their high horses and come back into the real world. If it's impossible to accept that teachers are human beings who occasionally let things slip or make mistakes, then they will simply have to replace us with robots. Surely a 'warts and all' inspection is better for everyone concerned?

In any case, the reality of any inspection is that it can only ever be a snapshot of a moment in time. Sadly for the inspectors, they most likely won't be there when those really magical lessons take place, when all of a sudden the class just seems to 'gel'. They probably won't get to see that wonderful lesson in which the children suddenly grasped that really tricky concept that you'd been battling to explain for weeks. Or the moment when you turn around a class that has been a night-mare all year.

Forget Ofsted, and remember what's really important: the children. You know yourself whether (despite the occasional off-day) on the whole you're a good and effective teacher.

What does it matter if Ofsted only rate you 'satisfactory' or worse? It's what the children think that counts.

For more information, or to look up an Ofsted report on a school of your choice, go to www.ofsted.gov.uk.

O is also for ...

Observations – Someone watching someone else's lesson, often for assessment purposes, but sometimes simply to see what happens. In my opinion, observations are the great missed chance when it comes to training teachers. I've been fortunate in that my work has offered me the chance to watch plenty of other teachers in action. By doing this, I've learned loads about what does and doesn't work in the classroom. I've been able to see how I might do things better myself and I've got some fantastic ideas for lessons. Observing other teachers at work allows you to nick all the best ideas that they have, and to understand better why some approaches just don't work.

PARENTS

The people who bring up a child, traditionally a mother and father.

In one way, parents make it possible for us to do our job. After all, without parents there wouldn't be any children, and consequently no need for teachers (or, for that matter, much chance for the future of the human race). In another way, some parents can make it almost impossible for us to do our job. The problem comes when parents bring up their children without even the most basic skills. Some children start school with little idea about how to behave, unable to speak or listen properly, or with poor concentration. This means that teachers spend the first few years of a child's education (or in some cases much longer) trying to undo the damage that has been done in those crucial first few years of life.

Like it or not, where education is seen increasingly as a business, parents are the 'customers' that we as teachers are trying to please. Consequently, it's worth getting to know the nature of the 'parent' beast. Parents come in three basic types. Type 'A' are those who don't want to contribute to their children's education at all, unless it involves coming into school to beat up the teacher for daring to set little Johnny a detention. Type 'B' are those who know our job better than we do, and who have no hesitation in telling us how to ensure that little Annie gets an A* at GCSE. Finally, type 'C' are the ones we love to work with – those parents who bring up their children properly and then support teachers in their quest to get on with the job of actually teaching them.

I used to regularly curse the parents who had 'dragged up' the children I had to teach. That was until I became a parent myself, and realized just what a difficult job it is to get right. I do often wonder why, despite the huge range of subjects in the curriculum, there is so little emphasis on the topic of 'how to be a good parent'. Perhaps there is a belief that parenting should come naturally, that it's something we are genetically hard-wired to be able to do. However, with the loss for many of the extended family, there are actually many people who have had little or no experience of babies and children until they have one of their own.

Good parenting is part of a cycle: we need a positive model to follow if we are going to do the job effectively. If a child is brought up badly, then they have nothing much to go on when it comes to working out how to bring up their own children. Some of our children have parents barely out of nappies themselves. Young parents will, of course, have relatively little experience of the world. If you become a parent before you even leave your teenage years, then you are probably going to feel resentment about not being able to go out, or about losing the chance to get out into the workplace and earn some money. Of course, some young parents bring up their children brilliantly, but it's important that we offer them the support that they need.

Making quality connections with the parents of the children you teach plays an important role in effective education. There are various ways in which you might build up good communication with parents. First and foremost, parents need to feel that they can actually contact the school if they have any questions or concerns. At early years' level, many teachers will have at least a passing contact with parents when they drop off their children at school. Here, the problem might be that too many demands are made on the teacher's time when he or she is trying to prepare for the day's teaching. In these instances, it can be a good idea to set up a formalized way of meeting parents, perhaps asking them to make appointments at a specific time.

At secondary level, much of the communication that does occur (and often, it's not much) will be at the formal parents' evening, and also through phone calls home. With a shortage of time, it can be tempting to limit your use of phone calls to times when things have gone badly wrong. However, the phone can be used in far more positive ways – to set up a series of targets for a child, or offered as a motivation for good behaviour (see 'Rewards').

Other ways in which contact can be established between the school and the home include building an active Parent-Teacher Association (PTA), or by inviting parents into the classroom as volunteers. Many parents do go into primary schools to assist with reading, but this technique is far less widely used within the secondary system.

It can sometimes feel like we are working against, rather than with, the parents of the children that we teach. Some parents will become aggressive or abusive towards staff, and this can lead to an increasing sense of 'them and us'. While you will have to accept that there are some parents who have little or no interest in their children's success, the vast majority will want to help out if you can only find ways to offer them the chance.

P is also for . . .

PTA – Parent-Teacher Association. A voluntary association that supports the school by raising money, organizing activities and generally creating positive links between home and school. As the name suggests, the membership will be made up of both parents and teachers.

Parents' evening – An evening at which parents can talk to teachers about their child's progress at school. If you are new to teaching, your first parents' evening will feel like a very scary experience. Always remember that old saying about snakes and spiders – they're more scared of you than you are of them. The same applies to the vast majority of the parents.

Pension – The money paid to a worker after he or she retires. In teaching, as in other public sector jobs, the pension is a real perk of the profession. For more information, see www. teacherspensions.co.uk (England and Wales), www.scotland. gov.uk/sppa/ (Scotland) and www.deni.gov.uk/teachers/ pensions/index.htm (Northern Ireland).

Personalized learning – Learning that is suited to the individual child. The latest 'great idea' is that children will learn best if the way that they are taught, and what they are actually taught, is personalized to their own individual learning styles. The idea apparently includes using ICT in some as yet undefined way. I suppose that this is the logical outcome of the current emphasis on learning styles and accelerated learning. (Some of that wonderfully named 'blue skies thinking' has obviously been going on at the DfES – it's the teachers who are left, once again, needing an umbrella as the initiatives rain down.) I know it's a long address to type, but you might like to read the following paper entitled 'Personalised Learning: The Emperor's Outfit?' at www.ippr.org.uk/research/files/team23/ project233/PL%20paper%20for%20publication.PDF.

Phonics – Learning to read by sounding out the letters and letter combinations. The debate about how children best learn to read has raged on for decades. A combination of phonics and context-based clues is now generally accepted to be the best approach.

Photocopying – Making a duplicate of a document on a photocopying machine. The Workload Agreement should, in theory, mean an end to the delights of the photocopying queue (which, for the benefit of the novice, is a line made up of increasingly frustrated people waiting behind a teacher who is copying an entire term's worth of worksheets). In some ways this is great – just think of all that extra free time. In other ways, though, we are losing the teachers' equivalent of the 'water-cooler moment': the chance to share an in-depth sociological debate with your fellow professionals. (Or in other words, the chance to have a chat about last night's edition of *Eastenders*.)

Pigeonhole – A small slot for post, usually located in the staffroom. The teacher's pigeonhole bears striking similarities to the letterbox found in the home. It is a slot into which all manner of papers are shoved. Some of these papers will be of vital importance; others will be completely meaningless. There are fun ones, such as the salary slip (the equivalent to receiving a cheque in the post); the statutory forms that must be completed (the equivalent of bills and tax returns); and the other myriad bits of meaningless paper (the teaching equivalent of junk mail). When you first become a teacher, having your very own name on your very own pigeonhole will be a source of immense joy. This very quickly disintegrates into a sinking feeling as you face that stack of papers once again.

Planning – Working out and writing down what you're going to teach before you actually teach it. Plans do not necessarily marry up exactly with the lessons that they are supposed to describe. This is not because teachers cannot follow instructions, but because it is almost impossible to work out how a lesson is going to run beforehand. The best teachers think on their feet and are willing to ditch a plan if it doesn't work. See also 'Lesson plans'.

PGCE – Post Graduate Certificate in Education. Does exactly what it says on the tin: a certificate, taken after you graduate, in the subject of education.

Praise – Giving a positive comment, whether written or spoken. Praise is an incredibly powerful tool in the world of the teacher, and yet it is free and easy to give. It can be as simple as saying 'well done', or 'great work' to a child.

Promotion – Moving into a post that is further up the teaching scale. If you're a good teacher, from the word go the pressure will be on you to try for promotion. If what you really love to do is teach, remember that any promotion will inevitably take your focus away from the day-to-day classroom job (unless you are applying for an AST post).

Pupils – The children who study at a school. The words 'pupils' and 'students' have different connotations. 'Pupil' tends to be used in more formal, traditional settings and to my ear has a slightly old-fashioned ring to it. 'Student' simply describes anyone who is studying.

QUESTION

To make a query or request, or to puzzle over something.

The asking and answering of questions plays a key role in the technique of the classroom teacher. A teacher might ask questions for a variety of reasons: to find out how much a class already knows about a subject, to work out where we need to go next, and what is still left to cover, or to tease out and develop the children's thoughts and responses.

The nature of our work means that we can get into the habit of asking questions when it's not actually the best approach to use. A great tip is never to use a question when you mean to get what you ask. The thinking is that it's not fair on the children to ask a question because you aren't actually offering them an option. So, don't meekly ask 'Would you mind getting rid of that paper aeroplane now please, David?' (at which point David instantly obeys by chucking his aeroplane across the room). Instead, use an accurate command statement such as 'I want you to put that paper down on the desk now, please, and get on with your work'.

The difference between open and closed questions provides a useful metaphor for differing attitudes to education. We might check whether a child can answer a closed question, such as

'What is the capital of England?' If the student is able to answer correctly, then we can say that she has learnt a certain piece of knowledge, and we can tick the relevant box to say what has been achieved. Open questions, on the other hand, require more time, more freedom, and less of a desire to quantify learning through acquiring a set of skills and facts. These open questions can lead to some great discussion work within a class, although they will inevitably take up more time and require you to be more flexible in your desire to 'get through the work'.

Being able to answer questions correctly and accurately becomes most important during the taking of an examination. You will probably have tried on numerous occasions to drum into your students the importance of actually answering the question that has been asked. Many children will be stumped by this requirement and will need your advice on how to actually go about doing it. A great tip is to get your students to use the question to frame their answer. This will help get them started and also keep them on track. For instance, a question in a history paper asks 'What factors led to the outbreak of the Second World War?' To start their answer, all the student needs to do is to turn that question into a statement as follows: 'A number of factors led to the outbreak of the Second World War. These factors were ...'

Finally, teachers do have a habit of using rhetorical questions, often with a hint of sarcasm in their voice. This includes the classic use of the question 'What did you say?' when a child swears. To which the answer 'I said you're a f★★★★★★ c★★★' could in fact be seen as a correct and accurate (if a rather rude) reply.

Q is also for ...

QCA – The Qualifications and Curriculum Authority. A public body that oversees the National Curriculum and related examinations, and which monitors college and work qualifications. See www.qca.org.uk for more information.

QTS – Qualified Teacher Status. A term describing someone who has passed the induction year and is consequently qualified to work as a teacher. See www.tta.gov.uk for more information.

Quiet – An extremely low level of noise. Teachers will sometimes ask a class for 'quiet' when what they actually mean is 'silence'. Finding precisely the right word to use might seem overly fussy, but it will enable your children to understand exactly what you mean.

Quit – To leave or give up, often with reference to a job. As a teacher it can, at times, be extremely tempting to shout 'I quit!' and storm out of your school. However, teaching has a particularly long notice period. In order to quit you will have to decide long in advance rather than on the spur of the moment. The exact dates are 31 October for the end of the Autumn term, 28 February for the end of the Spring term, and 31 May for the end of the Summer term.

Quiz – An informal game or competition in which correct answers must be given to questions. Quizzes are a staple feature of the last day of term. Using the format of a popular TV quiz can be very effective as it engages the children and gives them a structure within which to work. (Come to think of it, I'm sure that many teachers could outdo Anne Robinson with their vitriolic rendition of 'You are the weakest link, goodbye'.)

REWARDS

*Incentives given to increase motivation, for instance to encourage a
person to work harder or behave better.*

There are some children who come to school with an inner
motivation to work or behave well: they have been shown the
value of education for their own betterment, and they plan to
work hard to achieve their very best. They have high self-
esteem and high expectations of what they can do if they apply
themselves. This intrinsic motivation is not something that
happens overnight. It is built up over years of effective parenting, in which the child is taught to value him or herself as a
person, and is shown that learning can be its own reward.

On the other hand, many of the children that we teach do
not come equipped with this basic motivation to do well.
Instead, they need us to find and use effective rewards if they
are going to do as we wish. The well-chosen and well-targeted
reward is a powerful thing: it can switch an individual child or a
whole class back onto learning. Rewards are funny things,
though, and what works well in one class or with one student
will have absolutely no impact at all on another.

The area of rewards is a bit of a minefield for the unsuspecting teacher. There can be a tendency to end up rewarding

the badly behaved children, or those who refuse to work hard, simply to try and get them on side. Other dangers include using sweet things, because of the dubious message that this might send. In fact, in many circumstances the power of your approval is one of the best rewards of all. This will only work in a situation where the children are motivated to win your praise. For the child who has never been told how good he or she is before, then a simple 'well done' can be one of the most wonderful rewards of all.

For those children with a 'reputation' for being naughty to uphold, you may need to keep your rewards private. A passing comment in the corridor, such as 'great goal in the football yesterday' can have more impact than a bucket load of stickers.

I'd like to tell you Barry's story, to illustrate the power of a reward that is really, truly wanted. Barry was a tricky customer in a Year 8 English bottom set. The class had more than its fair share of children with special needs, and some of the students verged on the unteachable. By himself, Barry was nice enough, but he was really exacerbating the difficulties that I faced with that class.

The biggest problem was getting Barry to stay in his seat for more than thirty seconds at a time. He would settle his bottom on the chair for a split second, before setting off to wander the room. There was no aggressive intent in Barry's wandering, he was simply interested to see what everyone else was doing. I suspect that it was a work avoidance strategy. Barry found literacy hard and he probably figured that if he wandered the room with enough persistence I would simply give up on expecting him to actually produce any work. The problem was, though, that the other students were seeing this as a sign that they too could wander the room. By this stage my classroom looked like some kind of avant-garde dance performance.

I tried every strategy under my belt – from stickers to sanctions, from bribery to blackmail, but nothing seemed to work. By this stage I was getting desperate, and in my nightmares I was resorting to staple-gunning Barry to the chair.

At that point I turned in desperation to a member of the SEN staff to ask how I might motivate Barry to stay in his seat. 'What reward can I use to encourage him to behave properly?', I asked. It turned out that what Barry wanted, more than any-thing else in the world, was for his father to be pleased with him. If I could find a way to capitalize on the power of that relationship, it was likely that I could turn Barry's behaviour around.

So, at the start of the next lesson I took Barry to one side for a chat. 'You know how I need you to stay in your seat, Barry?', I asked. 'Well, I'm going to offer you a very good reward if you can manage to stay sat down for the whole lesson today.' 'What's that, miss?', Barry asked with a vague spark of interest in his eyes. 'I'm going to phone home after school today, and tell your dad how well you behaved for me.' Off Barry trotted, a big smile on his face. He stayed sat in his seat for the rest of the lesson, as though I had super-glued him to the chair.

That evening, I got Barry's home phone number and called his dad as promised. 'Is that Mr Chapman?', I asked, explaining who was calling. 'What's he done now?' the answer came. (A quick aside: Mr Chapman's response should perhaps tell us something about how we normally use phone calls home – to report poor behaviour.) Anyway, I told Barry's dad all about how well his son had done that day, and how pleased I was with him. I talked with him about how we could work together to improve Barry's behaviour and learning, and to set some targets for the future. (All the time I could hear little Barry chirping in the background, 'Is that Miss Cowley? What's she saying about me? I did good, didn't I dad?')

The next day Barry turned up at my lesson with a smile on his face. 'Will you phone my dad again tonight, miss?', he asked. At that point, concerned about a nightly regime of phone calls home, I told Barry that I would call home at the end of each week to report on his work and behaviour, and that simple offer was enough to keep him in line. At the next parents' evening, Mr Chapman came to speak to me with Barry in tow. It was a wonderful feeling for us all to talk about how Barry had turned his behaviour (and consequently his work) around.

Of course, teachers also need rewards. Obviously, we get the reward of a salary for turning up at school, but being a teacher is about much more than that. For many of us, the job is a reward in itself – the teacher who sees his or her job as a vocation will be rewarded daily with a high level of job satisfaction. We have the chance to develop strong and lasting relationships with our students, to spend all day every day working with the subjects that we love. And of course we have the opportunity to realize the biggest and most lasting reward of all – knowing that we've made a difference, no matter how small, to somebody else's life.

R is also for...

Reception – The first year of statutory schooling. As well as being a 'reception' into formal education, this can also be an age when children are at their peak of receptiveness to learning.

Register – A legal document in which the teacher marks the presence or absence of a child. Registers can be taken in the traditional 'green book' which, when you first receive it, makes you feel like a proper teacher at last. Alternatively, you might use SIMS reports, which are a computerized format produced on a single sheet of paper, on which the teacher puts a mark for absent or present. Some schools do use a completely computer-based system, in which the teacher uses a small laptop type machine on which to take the register. Of course, any computerized system will be subject to the vagaries of electronic equipment (i.e. there will inevitably be times when it doesn't work).

Relationships – The way that two or more people (or things) relate to each other. Being an effective teacher is all about building positive relationships with your children. In the primary school, you spend five days a week for a whole year with your class. This can be both positive and negative when it comes to developing relationships. On the plus side, you will spend enough time together to really get to know your children. On the minus side, you will spend so much time together that you will have to find ways to manage your relationship with any irritating or annoying individuals. In the secondary school, the amount of contact time with each student is much lower. In these circumstances, building positive relationships and partnerships with individuals or classes can be much more difficult. In every situation, to develop quality relationships the children will need to believe that you respect them as people, and that you are going to do everything in your power to help them to learn.

Reports – A written document which outlines how well a child is doing at school. When writing reports some teachers do find it hard to actually think up the phrases to use. For sets of subject specific comments to help you save time when writing reports, see www.educate.org.uk/teacher_zone/teaching/inschool/assess.htm.

Reputation – The opinion people have of you, based on prior experiences. Reputations are a very powerful thing within a school. As a newly qualified teacher you might look at the more experienced staff and wonder why on earth a class will behave perfectly for them, while stopping just short of a riot for you. The answer lies, at least partly, in the power of a good reputation. Reputations take a while to build up, but eventually a kind of Chinese whisper of good reports about your teaching will gain momentum, and your children will come to you already expecting good things. Of course, reputations are a double-edged sword – great if your reputation is a good one, but a nightmare if you are preceded by a bad reputation.

Resources – Any 'thing' that is used in school to help with learning. We tend to think of resources as being paper based – worksheets, lesson plans, text books and the like. But many of the best resources are actually rather more imaginative than this. You might bring some props in to 'kick start' a lesson or you could invite a parent or expert in to talk to the children. The more inventive the resources you use, the better results you will get from your class.

Retention – Hanging on to the teachers that the school already has. It is one of the ironies of teaching that the best schools will find it easy to retain good teachers, and consequently to stay on top of their game. Long-term relationships with the children can be built, teachers and other staff can work well together, and so on. The 'worst' schools, those where behaviour is poor, morale is low, or staff support is inadequate, will find it much harder to hang on to good staff. This becomes a vicious cycle whereby the children never see the same faces for long, and consequently never develop the sense of trust required for good work or behaviour.

Risk assessment – Working out the potential for danger before it has actually happened. The tendency in modern society is increasingly to assess the risk of everything we do. The fact that schools and local authorities are more and more likely to be sued when something goes wrong contributes to this. I had to laugh when I talked to a head teacher recently, who was about to spend many hours filling out risk assessments for every aspect of her school environment. She had to identify the possible dangers of going to the toilet – could a tile become cracked, and if it did, what potential danger would this mean? It strikes me that we might want to ask ourselves whether this is the most positive use of a senior manager's time?

S IS FOR . . .

SUPPLY TEACHER

A temporary teacher brought in to cover the absence of the usual teacher.

When it comes to supply teachers, I'm fortunate in that I am able to view the subject from both sides. I've seen the bombsite that used to be my classroom the day after I went out on an INSET course, and wondered how on earth such a mess could possibly be made in only five hours. (Actually, although it's common to blame the supply teacher for this, in fact it is sometimes your fellow members of staff who have failed to respect your teaching space.) I've also worked as a supply teacher, and had to cope with all the difficulties that come with the job.

Being a supply teacher is possibly the hardest teaching job there is, especially if you're doing day-to-day supply in a range of different schools. It's a bit like being Bill Murray in the film *Groundhog Day*. Over and over again you feel like a new teacher on the first day of term in a really tough school. If you've never done supply, please don't be too hard on those supply teachers that come into your school or your classroom. The supply teacher really is up against it: there are a whole host of difficulties with which we have to contend.

For a start, as a supply teacher you simply don't know who anyone is (staff or children). And kids being kids they are inclined to give the wrong name if they get into trouble. Just like when a teacher first starts at a school, the poor supply has no clue how the systems at the school work, for instance which sanctions and rewards should be used. Sometimes, none of this information will be forthcoming unless a direct request is made for it. (At which point, the deputy involved will disappear, saying 'I'll just go and make you a photocopy', never to be seen again.)

The kids do constantly try it on when they have a supply teacher. It never ceases to amaze me the number of schools at which the children are supposedly 'allowed' to wear coats and trainers or use their mobile phones in class. The children tend to have the (fairly understandable) attitude that a lesson with a supply teacher 'doesn't count', and that having a supply teacher equals a lesson or a day off.

The supply teacher must also find his or her way around from scratch. This can mean spending the whole of break trying to locate the staff toilets, only to discover that, having eventually found them, a secret code is required for entry. Of course, at this point the bell will ring for the end of break.

Inside the classroom, supply teachers often have to teach outside their subject and in a number of different teaching areas. On arriving at the lesson, he or she will often find that much of the work that has been left will be, not to put too fine a point on it, total crap. (I can say this, because despite my best intentions I've been guilty of leaving crap work for supply teachers when I was in a permanent job. I know how it goes – you've phoned in feeling terrible, or you're rushing off home on the night before an INSET course with no time to spare.) On many occasions, the children will have (a) done the work before, (b) finished it in the last lesson, or (c) find it hopelessly boring or impossibly difficult.

Here are some top tips for supply teachers, based on my own experiences of doing the job. First of all, make sure that you're armed with all the information you need. I find that details about any reward systems can be particularly useful. I regularly start my lessons by waving a reward slip at a class, and saying

'I've got three of these to give out today, so let's see who wants to earn them'. Although it might seem tempting to be quite relaxed with your classes, in the hope of getting them on your side, I find that conversely it's actually important to set the standards high.

Try to make the first thirty seconds count. Faced with a supply teacher, the children will be making a snap judgement about whether or not you are going to be any good. You need to make that first impression count – to show that you are going to be strong, positive and in control. Pick up on any small infringements – you want coats off, ties done up correctly, students sitting properly in their seats. Dealing with these relatively minor misdemeanours will send the message that you mean business. If behaviour in the school is halfway decent, I will even insist that a class lines up outside the room before I let them in.

Sometimes you will find yourself in the horrible situation where a class simply refuses to listen to you introduce the lesson. If this happens to you, there is very little point in getting angry and shouting. Instead, try saying 'If you want to learn, come to the front'. This allows you to form a kind of 'pact' with the well-motivated kids, whereby you can insist that they actually do some work. (Perhaps surprisingly, when I have used this technique in the past, it has resulted in the vast majority of the class coming to listen, and around three truly disaffected youths entertaining themselves at the back of the room.)

To overcome the 'wrong name' syndrome, you might like to take in a digital camera. Promising that a photograph will be shown to the relevant senior manager is usually enough for the child to miraculously remember his or her own name. In the past I have also made use of my mobile in a game of bluff, pretending to phone the school reception and asking to be put through to the head teacher to discuss the class's behaviour.

When things do go well, it is hard to know whether it is your skill as a teacher, or simply that you're teaching a reasonably nice class. Pleasingly, I was once presented with the proof that my strategies were working. At the end of a Year 9 drama class, one student approached me for a chat. 'I don't know what you did, miss,' she said, 'but usually we're really horrible even to our teachers and you managed to get us doing lots of work and behaving really well.' As she walked away with a puzzled look on her face, I allowed myself a small pat on the back.

So, next time you curse supply teachers from the comfortable position of your permanent job, bear in mind that the day might come when you too have to face the *Groundhog Day* life of the supply.

S is also for . . .

Sanctions – Punishments given at school for poor behaviour or inadequate work. The 'big stick' of sanctions will only work if the students don't want to receive the punishments that we give.

Scheme of work – An overview of the lessons that are going to be covered during the study of a particular topic.

SIMS – School Information Management System. A software package which provides information management for schools. You may have come across SIMS registers, on which the teacher makes a mark to indicate the presence or absence of a child, and a computer correlates the results.

Selection – Choosing which students can come to a school on the basis of ability or other criteria. Schools which do decide to select by ability will inevitably achieve good examination results, making them popular with parents and consequently over-subscribed.

Self-evaluation – Examining your own practice to see how effectively you are doing your job. The ability to self-evaluate is vital in becoming a reflective teacher. The very best teachers are able to evaluate what they do as they actually teach, subtly adapting their lesson format, content and delivery to suit the mood and responses of the class.

SMT – Senior Management Team: a group of senior managers who oversee the running of the school, typically the head and one or more assistant or deputy heads. In schools with a more 'touchy-feely' approach, the SMT are often known as the SLT, or Senior Learning Team.

Setting – Dividing the children up according to their ability, often in a particular subject area. There are various points for and against setting children. On the plus side, it means that the work can be better suited to the students' abilities, with less need for differentiation because of the similar levels within the group. Behaviour tends to be good in top sets, but conversely, bottom sets, with many children who have special needs, can be very challenging to teach. If a student is placed in the wrong set this can also lead to difficulties: both for the child and the teacher.

Shouting – The teacher making loud use of his or her voice. Some teachers see shouting as a form of sanction – 'Because I shout at them they're scared of me and they behave themselves.' On the other hand, shouting can also be a form of reward for some children – at least they are receiving some sort of attention. On the whole, shouting doesn't work as a behaviour management strategy, because it shows that the class can make the teacher lose control of him or herself. In addition, teachers who shout regularly are putting an unhealthy strain on their voices. See also 'Voice'.

Slang – An informal language used within a specific group of people. Using slang is attractive to young people because it can keep other people from understanding what they are saying. Slang changes rapidly: for instance the word 'cool' has now mutated into 'bad' or 'wicked'. Teachers are strongly advised against trying to use slang to get 'in' with the kids – it will probably backfire and leave you sounding like a fool.

SEN – Special Educational Needs. A child who has special needs in relation to his or her education, who finds it more difficult to learn than other children of the same age, and who will need extra support to access the curriculum. The child's needs may be due to a range of factors: a physical disability, a hearing or sight impairment, a medical condition, an emotional or behavioural difficulty, a general or specific learning difficulty, or a speech or language problem.

Special measures – A school is put into 'special measures' after an Ofsted inspection if it is 'failing or likely to fail to give its pupils an acceptable standard of education' (Schools Inspections Act 1996). It is the educational equivalent of putting a school on a life support machine.

Staffroom – A room within the school where staff congregate to relax, drink coffee, complain about their classes, curse the SMT, do a bit of marking and generally escape from the kids.

SATs – Standard Assessment Tasks. These are government tests in English, Maths and Science. They are taken at the end of Key Stage 1 (Year 2), the end of Key Stage 2 (Year 6) and the end of Key Stage 3 (Year 9).

Stress – The feeling that you cannot cope with the pressures and demands placed upon you, leading to emotional or psychological strain.

Student teacher – A person studying to become a teacher.

Study leave – Time spent off school, supposedly studying, before exams. There are plans afoot to curtail or even stop study leave. I'm sure that the statistics are right when they show how students who don't go on study leave do much better in their exams, but this actually misses the point. Study leave isn't for the students, it's for the teachers, isn't it? It turns the end of the summer term into a time of the year when we can catch up on all those little jobs that never get done; when we can go on a course that interests us, and so on.

T IS FOR . . .

TRIPS

Time spent out of school, visiting a place of educational value.

A trip is possibly one of the best experiences any child will have during his or her school career. For some children, the chance to go on a field trip, or to the theatre, or just to the local park, is something completely missing from their normal everyday lives. The educational value of the school trip should not be underestimated: although the learning that takes place is not easily measured, the inspiration and increased motivation that come out of a trip can be truly wonderful to see. Sadly, though, trips are being increasingly curtailed because of fears over the risk factors of venturing out into the 'real world'.

Longer residential trips bring with them the opportunity for plenty of mischief. The students have a real sense of fun and excitement, and being out of their normal school environment means that it can be tempting for them to push at the boundaries. Kids being kids, there will almost inevitably be secretive attempts at drinking and smoking from older students (and some of the younger ones as well). Teachers are obviously responsible for the children's safety when they are on a trip. However, it can pay to be a little bit more accepting about the reality of the modern teenager. There are numerous tales about trips stored in my bank of teacher anecdotes. One of the more amusing is the story of the courting sixth formers who were discovered in the same room after lights out. I'll leave the details up to your imagination.

Just one more thought on the subject of trips: perhaps it says something that 'getting out of school' for the day is the best thing that can happen to our students? Perhaps we should aim to find ways of actually making going into school and staying there as vital and exciting as getting out. If we could do this, then perhaps our children might be more inclined to work and behave as we would wish?

T is also for . . .

TTA – The Teacher Training Agency. A public body involved in the recruitment and training of teachers. See www.tta. gov.uk for more information.

Teaching assistant – An assistant who works with the teacher to help support the children's learning. The role of teaching assistants is a controversial one at the moment. Some teachers feel that letting an assistant actually teach a lesson to a whole class will undermine the professional credibility of the qualified teacher.

TP – Teaching Practice. Time spent in school and in the classroom while training to be a teacher. Students will spend a substantial amount of time in school during their teacher training. The learning that is done 'on the job' during TP is invaluable in the process of becoming a teacher. On a PGCE course, a substantial part of the academic year will be spent on TP. This can pile on the pressure (although bear in mind that you will have nothing like the full responsibilities of a permanent member of staff). On a BEd/BA QTS degree, the TPs will be more spaced out, and there will be time between each one to reflect on the progress made.

Texting – Sending text messages from one mobile phone to another, typically using abbreviated language. Those children who you see staring into their laps during the lesson could well be composing texts the length of *War and Peace*. It's time for teachers to re-appropriate texting for themselves. You might use it as a way of sending reminders about homework, or of communicating with a child who is absent from school.

Times Educational Supplement – The teachers' bible, known colloquially as the 'TES' and published every Friday. If you teach at a school where the job sections disappear before the first period of the day, this is a good indicator that many of your colleagues are planning to escape.

Timetable – The timing of lessons during the school day/week. The primary school teacher will usually have some flexibility in deciding on how his or her timetable is run (for instance deciding the times that specific subjects will be taught). In the secondary school, the teacher will be handed a timetable and expected to get on with it. Before cursing the creator of your timetable for that horrible Tuesday with five periods of nightmare Year 9, do accept that creating a timetable for a large secondary school is a very complex business.

In some schools the timetable might run across a fortnight rather than a week, with some subjects being timetabled once every fourteen days. (This can lead to some children turning up late for lessons or without the correct equipment – 'But I thought it was Week A!') I once taught in a school with a six day timetable. Although this was confusing at first for both teachers and students, it actually worked very well. Rather than being stuck with teaching a specific class last thing every Friday (never a recipe for high motivation), these 'graveyard slots' would rotate around each week.

Trust – Having faith in someone or something. In teaching, trust (or the lack of it) is an integral part of our work. There is the trust that we have to have in our students if we are to encourage them to be responsible citizens; there is also the lack of trust that various governments have demonstrated about teachers as thinking professionals.

UNIFORM

A set of clothes worn to indicate that a child attends a particular school.

The choices that a school makes about uniform can be a good indicator of the head teacher's general attitude towards education. In a school which views itself as 'promoting traditional standards', a strict uniform code will probably be in existence. These strict uniform codes do tend to be popular with parents, who show a remarkable amnesia about their own school days and the uniforms that they most likely hated. In a school that prefers to put good relationships and effective learning at the top of the agenda, the children's comfort will be of most importance. Where enforcing a uniform code might lead to confrontations, some schools will sensibly do away with it altogether.

Part of the point about a uniform is that it takes away individuality – it makes each child equal, at least in terms of appearance. Of course, by their very nature, kids will always find ways to overcome this and to personalize their uniforms to hint at rebellion and individuality. (Although conversely, their uniform-personalization will typically be a school-wide phenomenon, in which being 'part of the crowd' is actually a key part of the agenda.) These days, there seems to be a fashion for doing up ties with a tiny 'fat bit' in front of the knot, and a huge long 'skinny' bit dangling down inside the shirt. On occasions where I'm feeling particularly strict, I take great delight in getting them to unknot and retie their ties in the correct manner. In my own school days there was a fad for tucking our school jumpers into our skirts, for the skinny girls at least.

With the obvious potential for mess involved in teaching young children, primary schools seem good at fitting the uniform to its purpose, and also ensuring that it is comfortable to wear. A typical primary uniform might feature a loose polo shirt, a sweatshirt with a school crest, and a specific colour of trousers or skirt. At secondary level, there seems to be much more emphasis on a more traditional type of uniform, with ties, blazers and even hats still in evidence at many schools. Any uniform that features a boater (remember those?) as part of its requirements is by definition from a private school.

The poor teacher is, as usual, at the sharp end of things when it comes to getting the students to actually comply with uniform requirements. Depending on the school, demands of 'Put your blazer/tie on please' might be met with surly compliance or downright refusal. Although it can at times seem rather pointless to be strict over uniform (surely it's their learning that we're worried about, not their appearance), in fact clamping down on small infringements can give the signal that this is a teacher who means business.

Although I was not especially rebellious as a child, I did object strongly when the innocuous blue blazer worn at my own secondary school was changed to one featuring a putrid shade of green. Luckily, I was able to use my 'impoverished single parent family' status to great effect. Having an older sister who had worn a blue blazer, my mum was happy to write me a note to the effect that we couldn't afford a new one and that, like it or not, I was going to wear my sister's blue one until it fell apart. So it was that, while my contemporaries were teased mercilessly by the kids from the other local comp, I could blend into the background in my cast-off blazer.

The issue of uniform makes an excellent topic for debate in the classroom. On the plus side, it gives a sense of belonging and identity to the students. It is a great equalizer – it means that they don't need to try to outdo each other with the latest designer gear. On the negative side, uniforms can be uncomfortable and depersonalizing. Uniforms can also lead to trouble where there are conflicts between the children in different local schools. I have a vivid memory of walking down the road after school one day with a group of friends in their green blazers (I was in blue, see above). A huge gang of kids from the rival school suddenly appeared in the distance. My friends were immediately identified as the green-blazered enemy, and the ensuing race to safety probably broke the record for the four minute mile.

While on the subject of uniforms, what is it with children and trainers? If I had a pound for every note I have received insisting that a student must wear trainers because of some unspecified foot disorder, I would be a very rich woman. (And in any case, I don't see how wearing thick sweaty trainers can be all that much better for their feet.) When I had a Year 11 tutor group one year, I would spend the vast majority of tutor time each morning going round the classroom to catch the trainer wearing crowd. Any refusal to comply with my 'put your shoes on' request would lead to an offer that I would 'play mummy' and do it for them. Thankfully no one took me up on the offer.

I recently saw a great idea for getting kids out of their trainers. The school invested in a number of those especially horrible plimsoles (you know the ones, we all wore them in the 'pre-trainer' years). Any student who arrived at school with trainers on, and without his or her shoes, had to wear the plimsoles instead. It cannot be denied that the embarrassment factor inherent in this punishment would very quickly make them comply.

U is also for . . .

Umpteen – Lots of something. As in 'I'm asking you for the umpteenth time not to stab Jimmy with your protractor.'

Underachievement – Not achieving what you could. It is

very frustrating to watch a child underachieving in his or her work. For the student who regularly fails to achieve what he or she could, try to find out the cause of the underachievement. Is it that the work seems irrelevant or boring, or is it perhaps at the wrong level for the student's ability? Are there any environmental factors impinging on the student's ability to work – cramped desks, room too hot/cold, etc.? Could it be that the child needs to be moved to another position in the room, either to avoid distractions from friends, or perhaps to see the board more easily?

Unions – Organizations which represent the workers in a particular job or profession. There are a number of different teaching unions and, although there is no compunction for teachers to join, these unions do offer good back-up, support and advice. They also offer an independent campaigning 'voice' for the profession. The unions are listed below in alphabetical order, with their website addresses.

- ATL (Association of Teachers and Lecturers): www.askatl.org.uk.
- NAHT (National Association of Head Teachers): www.naht.org.uk.
- NASUWT (National Association of Schoolmasters, Union of Women Teachers): www.teachersunion.org.uk.
- NATFHE (National Association of Teachers in Further and Higher Education): www.natfhe.org.uk.
- NUT (National Union of Teachers): www.teachers.org.uk.
- PAT (Professional Association of Teachers): www.pat.org.uk.
- SSTA (Scottish Secondary Teachers' Association): www.ssta.org.uk.
- SHA (Secondary Heads' Association): www.sha.org.uk.

Unwind – To relax, to shrug off your worries. In a stressful job, the ability to unwind will be crucial for your long-term health. Teachers find a variety of ways of winding down, some healthy, some less so. Perhaps surprisingly, a physical activity such as swimming can offer a good way of shrugging off the worries of the day. A trip down the pub on a Friday can also provide an effective, although not particularly healthy, way to relax. The start of the holidays can be a time when it proves particularly difficult to unwind. If you find this is the case for you, it could be a good idea to actually devote the first few days to getting all that work out of the way. (Work which will otherwise sit and look at you in a guilt-inducing way for the rest of the break.)

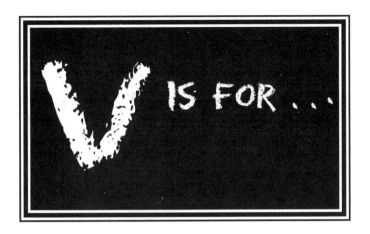

VOICE

Making sounds to communicate or contribute, speaking words or singing.

As a profession, teachers rely more heavily on their voices than almost any other. Even actors will only have to perform for a relatively short time each day. In the classroom, we are constantly using our voices to communicate with the children. This means that the subject of 'voice', and its correct and effective usage, is of crucial importance to the teacher.

First and foremost, we use our voices to do a million things in the classroom. We might be talking about a new topic, explaining a task, giving instructions, organizing the children into groups, giving feedback on a piece of work, explaining a reward or sanction, or setting homework. We also use our voices to express ourselves to the class. This might involve discussing our feelings and emotions in relation to the students, talking to build positive relationships with them, demonstrating our control or status, or establishing a teaching style. (Of course, it might also mean screaming 'Will you all just shut up!?')

I think it's fair to say that, on the whole, teachers do love the sound of their own voices. Not literally: if you tape record yourself teaching a lesson you will probably cringe at the way you sound. But we do love to explain things – that's often part of why we became a teacher in the first place. There is always that lurking danger that we spend too much time telling the class everything we want them to know, rather than getting them to learn via discovery.

Of course, as well as the teacher having a 'voice' in the classroom, the students will also have their own vocal contributions to make. In fact, at times it can seem like all they are doing is chatting to each other. Giving your children the opportunity to express their feelings or opinions, or to make their own contributions to the running of your classroom, plays a key part in establishing a good working partnership. The pressures of the curriculum can mean that we don't devote enough time to the simple pleasures of talking.

In many ways, teaching is akin to acting. We take on the role of the teacher, and perform daily to our audience of children (who are a hell of a lot harder to please than your standard theatre goers). The ability to act as different characters is a great boon to the teacher. This is especially so when it comes to using our voices to communicate our feelings to the class: we have the most wonderful opportunity to 'ham it up' by making effective use of tone.

You might talk in a very concerned or worried voice, letting the class know how disappointed you are with some behaviour. You could speak in a very enthusiastic way to get the students excited about a piece of work. You might read a story using a range of different voices and accents.

We can also use our voices as a way of keeping or gaining control of a class, and this is where the use of pace comes in handy. It might mean slowing down your voice to calm the children; it could mean speeding it up to create a sense of interest and excitement in the work. Combining different paces works well too – for instance, a sharp 'Right!' followed by a gradually slowing down 'I want you all to stop working and look this way, please'.

Our voices can also let us down on occasions: they can be treacherous, unfaithful friends. As you watch a class spin out of control, your voice may betray emotions of apprehension or frustration, anger or embarrassment. Learning how to segregate your actual emotions from the sound that comes out of your mouth is a skill that the teacher must learn early.

Of course, as well as considering the sound of what we say, we should also take into account the words that actually come out of our mouths. The hurly burly of the average classroom means that we will often speak without carefully considering what we are saying. However, it is important to think about the way that our words are likely to be perceived or interpreted by the children. Much comes down to semantics: to the specific meanings and intentions of the words we use. We need to be as accurate as possible, because this will have an impact on how our children work and behave.

For instance, when specifying the behaviour and attitudes you want from your children, try to frame what you say in a positive, rather than negative, way. The key is to ask for what you *do* want, rather than what you don't, because this helps build and maintain a positive atmosphere in your class. Instead of saying there should be 'no talking', you might say that the children 'must be silent when the teacher (or anyone else) is talking'. Accuracy of word usage is important as well – children do tend to take what we say very literally. If you ask for 'quiet', then that is what you will probably get. On the other hand, if you ask for 'silence', you will hopefully be able to hear the proverbial pin drop.

It's worth bearing in mind that minimizing your use of voice will often maximize the good behaviour you receive. I'm a great believer in the power of the pause in the classroom. As you start to talk to the class, you notice that a couple of students aren't listening. Instead of spotlighting their behaviour to the whole group, simply 'freeze' what you're saying and take a pause. The misbehaving students will (hopefully) turn to look why you've stopped, at which point you can give them the benefit of your icy glare before continuing.

Despite the fact that the voice is so vital to the teacher, there has historically been a lack of detailed professional training in voice usage. Taking proper care of our voice is clearly crucial – without it we cannot teach effectively. Problems with a teacher's voice can be born out of a number of different factors. For a start, simply having to talk all day every day will obviously put a strain on our voice, especially if we are not using it properly. Other culprits include dry atmospheres, a lack of time to keep properly hydrated, and also all those superbugs that roam the school corridors, giving us constant colds and infections.

The environments in which we teach are not necessarily conducive to making the best use of our voice. Poor classroom acoustics may mean that there is excessive background noise when the children are talking, or that we have to speak loudly to be heard. Teachers of practical subjects can be especially vulnerable. From the poor PE teacher who has to shout instructions across the field; to the drama teacher who must teach in a large, dry studio.

The tips for correct voice usage are easy to give, but much harder to follow when you're under the typical stresses of a teaching job. If at all possible, aim to warm up your voice by humming – you might even try this with the whole class as a novel 'starter activity'. Try to keep relaxed, maintain a good posture when speaking and breathe from your diaphragm. Remember to drink lots of water during your lessons (research has shown that getting your children to drink water too is a great aid to concentration). Learn to make use of other sounds apart from your voice. This might mean making a loud noise to gain the class's attention, for instance banging a table, dropping something or using a whistle. A great idea is to have a recognized 'I want silence' command, such as hands up or something more imaginative if you like.

Always remember that your voice plays a really vital role in the impression that other people have of you. Just think how the voices of various famous politicians help create an image in your mind. The irritatingly pregnant pauses of Tony Blair's speeches; the icy tones of the 'iron lady', Margaret Thatcher; the inadequate vocal strains of Iain Duncan Smith. As a teacher, your children will be forming their impressions of you from the moment that you first open your mouth.

V is also for...

Value-added – The 'value' which is 'added' to a child's level of ability by a school. The league tables now take account of how schools add value. Has it ever struck you how so many of the terms used in teaching seem to suggest that our children are some type of supermarket product?

Video – The 'educational video' is a great lifesaver for tired teachers. In the English department I always saw myself as extremely lucky to be able to justify showing full length productions of Shakespeare and other texts. These would take at least three if not four lessons to watch. Of course the downside of using video is the virtual guarantee that, despite all your careful checks, the machine will refuse to work.

Vocation – A job for which you feel completely suited: one to which you are happy to devote time and energy, or one that gives you so much satisfaction that you would almost do it for no financial reward at all. If that sounds like your view of the teaching profession, then you've made a great choice of career.

WORKSHEETS

Pieces of paper given to students, containing exercises, questions or instructions.

There are plenty of good reasons for using worksheets in the classroom. For a start, it is reasonably easy to create a worksheet on a computer, even if you are not particularly IT-literate. Once a basic worksheet has been created, it can be saved with small adaptations to help you differentiate for children with different levels of ability. Over the years, you will develop a 'bank' of previous worksheets that have worked well for you, and these can be reused with any minor adaptations as required.

Worksheets are also a good 'cop out' for when you just don't have the energy for any active teaching. In these circumstances, slapping a worksheet down in front of the kids and saying 'get on with it' can offer a lifeline to the tired teacher. If you're off school on a course, or if you have to phone in sick, setting a worksheet for the students to complete will overcome any issues about finding textbooks or other equipment. They can also be helpful towards the end of term when you would like to do some short, one-off fun activities. My experience suggests that children, especially those at the lower end of the ability range, do love those 'fill in the blanks' style worksheets or ones featuring wordsearches.

Despite all the benefits, there are of course dangers in using too many worksheets. Lesson after lesson of worksheeting will quickly leave the children bored and disaffected. The class will also suss out pretty quickly that you're being lazy. With the worksheet comes the danger that some children will finish the work within the first five minutes, and give you grief for the rest of the lesson when you try to persuade them to pad out their answers a little.

When designing worksheets, it's worth following a few basic tips to make sure they are easy to use. For students with low level literacy skills, it can be difficult to read a worksheet if it is heavily text based. Keep your presentation clear and simple, incorporating pictures or diagrams if you can. Use a text box or highlighting for important instructions and put this at or near the top so that it's the first thing they will see. If you are going to include a number of activities on the sheet, then put a summary of these at the top so that the children have a clear idea of each task that must be done. Making sure that your worksheets are beautifully presented with visual aids will help interest and motivate your students. If you're using the Microsoft Word program, then go to the Format button on your toolbar, click on 'Borders and Shading', then on 'Page Border' and look at the 'Art' options.

W is also for …

Whole-school behaviour policy – A document that outlines the way in which a school aims to manage behaviour. This document typically includes an outline of the school ethos, a list of school and classroom rules, details of rewards and sanctions, systems for dealing with confrontation, and so on. Although policies can sometimes be a meaningless waste of trees, when it comes to behaviour, the whole-school behaviour policy will be your bible. A good behaviour policy will be a lifeline for the teacher, who can use it as a formalized way of managing mis-behaviour. A decent policy will be one designed in conjunction with staff and students. It will be subject to regular change and review, to reflect the changing nature of any school. It will also be fully backed up by senior staff (not just in words, but in actions). In addition, the ideas and systems within the policy must actually work in real life situations.

Wordprocessing – Creating a text-based document on a computer. Wordprocessing software can offer a lifeline for the hard-pressed teacher. It can make the creation and adaptation of worksheets simpler, and their presentation more effective. It can also make writing reports a relatively straightforward matter.

Work/life balance – The balance between the type and amount of work a person does and the time available for other aspects of life. The subject of how teachers can achieve a reasonable 'work/life balance' plays an integral part in the current Workload Agreement. One of the problems with the job of the teacher is that there is no obvious end to the amount of work that could usefully be done. There will always be the option to do that little bit more, to stretch that little bit further, so that you can help your children learn. Finding a healthy balance between work life and home life is a key lesson to be learned in the first few years of your career.

Workload – The amount of work that a person must do. It's blindingly obvious to anyone who has ever been a teacher that it is not a nine-to-five job. While most teachers have no real problem with working fairly long hours, what they do resent is having their time squandered on meaningless tasks. So much of our time is spent on activities other than teaching – some useful, some a complete waste of time.

XMAS

Abbreviation for Christmas, a religious festival celebrated on 25 December.

Christmas is a great time of year to be a teacher. After the long hard slog of the first term, there comes a point about three weeks from the end when it is suddenly 'all down hill' to the holidays. With external exams still distant on the horizon, the build-up to Christmas time tends to be full of fun activities and creative endeavours. In the primary school, there is the traditional artistic task of making snowflakes or lanterns by snipping bits out of a folded piece of paper. Even in the secondary school the teacher might feel inspired to relax the hard work ethic a bit and set some fun and creative work to finish off the term.

Of course, there are also the joys of the Christmas play to be endured. For the poor primary school teacher, having to organize children from all different year groups into a semblance of a show can be the cause of premature white hairs. Images of school nativity plays feature regularly on video disaster shows such as *You've been Framed*. You know the ones I mean: Mary hitting Joseph over the head with Baby Jesus or the sheep toppling domino like off the bench on which they are standing.

In some of the schools where I have taught, there has been a tradition of putting on a staff Christmas Panto for the students (probably to the eternal regret of the poor head teachers, who are mercilessly dragged up for some ritual humiliation during the course of the show). The really great thing about a staff panto is that it shows the children that teachers are capable of letting their hair down a bit once in a while. Although it requires considerable effort to prepare, with the loss of lunch breaks for a good few weeks beforehand, the looks on the kids' faces when they see a teacher in drag are truly something wonderful to behold.

If you don't yet have a staff panto at your school, I would strongly recommend that you try to instigate this tradition. To give you just a taste of what you might expect, at one school that year's panto was based on the film *Men in Black*, but with a twist – this was *Men in Pink*. When the students saw their favourite geography teacher running up the aisle dressed in a pink miniskirt, fishnets and stilettos, the hall went wild. It was the talk of the school long after the Christmas season was over.

YOU

Referring to a person.

Teaching is very much an individual activity: it's all about *you*. Of course it matters how well-run and supportive a school is, how good the policies and systems are, and how strongly the parents support their children's learning. But at the end of the day the individual teacher plays the key role in running the classroom and educating the class.

Teaching can actually be quite a lonely job. Although more and more these days we have other adults in the classroom (particularly in the primary school), teaching is still essentially an individual activity. Everything about you will contribute to the success or otherwise of your students. What you say and do; the quality of your lesson planning and delivery; the way you manage the class, the space and the time; even the way that you appear. All these factors are parts of you that add up together to make the teacher that you are.

A great deal of the so-called 'art' of being a teacher is about an individual's ability to slog it out every single day of your teaching life. I have huge amounts of respect for those teachers who have managed to stick it in the classroom for years and years. Refusing to submit to cynicism (well, mostly), they devote their working lives to a difficult yet rewarding job. When we first come into the profession, with huge quantities of enthusiasm and energy, some of these 'old hands' might appear to be simply treading water in their careers. However, once the reality of what teaching involves hits home, you will quickly come to respect anyone who has put more than ten years' service into the profession.

Some teachers are naturals who have the ability to manage their children easily, and at the same time truly inspire them as well. Watch these teachers at work whenever you can – learn from them and try to understand what it is that makes them so successful. At the end of the day, though, you will have to find your own way, your own teaching style, your own particular version of 'you' the teacher.

ZEN

A state of calm and relaxation, refusing to worry about things that cannot be changed.

The poem 'If' kind of sums up what the 'zen' of teaching is all about. It's that line about keeping your head while everyone else is losing theirs. What you're aiming for is to be the calm centre in the middle of any storm that hits your classroom. No matter what is happening around you, the ability to stay centred and contained will serve you well. One of the big sources of stress for teachers is the emotional reactions stirred up by so many of those little day-to-day incidents. The minute you allow your emotions to take control, you will not be able to react rationally and calmly to the problems that you face.

Staying in this calm and relaxed state is not easy (particularly when 4K are winding you up tighter than a ball of string). There are various strategies that I have developed over the years, and I hope that some of these will help you to attain a centred and self-contained manner in your own classroom. For a start, try to build an invisible barrier around you, through which no abuse or misbehaviour can hit. It's a bit like the deflector shields on the Starship Enterprise – don't let those alien attacks get through your defences.

Learn to see difficult behaviour as the children's problem, not yours. Keep it in mind that any child who is abusive towards another person (let alone an adult in a supposed position of authority) must be going through some pretty horrible stuff in his or her own life. Pity rather than anger is the appropriate and professional response.

It's worth learning a few meditative techniques if you're planning to stay in teaching for the long term. These will help you keep your blood pressure and heart rate down. Breathe deeply, count to ten, pick a spot on the wall at which to stare, whatever works for you. In fact, many of these meditative techniques are useful for creating a zen-like atmosphere in your classroom, so why not incorporate some of them into your lessons so that your children can learn to be 'zen' as well? (See 'Concentration' for some more thoughts about this.)

The teacher who has mastered the 'zen' of teaching will appear fully in control of him or herself in front of the class. As the storm rages all around, this teacher will simply let problems slide off his or her back, like water off the proverbial duck. And who knows, perhaps a little of your calming influence might just rub off on the children?

Z is also for . . .

Zany – A bit mad, eccentric or surprising. When asked to describe what I'm like as a teacher, my students have often resorted (with a pitying look) to saying 'Well, you're a bit mad, miss, aren't you?' I have to say that I take this as a compliment. Thinking back to my own best teachers as a child, they all had one thing in common – they were a bit 'off-the-wall', a little bit weird and zany.

Zone – An area or place. The term being 'in the zone' is sometimes used to describe a person who is completely at one with what they are doing (a sculptor fixed on carving from a block of stone or a racing driver speeding around the Formula One track). The word zone can also be used in relation to a child who, despite their bodily presence in your classroom, appears to have mentally left the room. As the classic cliché goes, 'the lights are on but no one's home'. It must feel quite safe in the zone – disconnected from everything that is going on in the real world. Children will typically zone out when either (a) the teacher is nagging them endlessly and they're beyond caring, or (b) they are completely unable to comprehend what the hell the teacher is trying to teach them.

Zoo – A place where wild animals are kept so that people can visit them. Teachers will quite frequently use the zoo as a metaphor for their feelings about behaviour in their classrooms. 'It's like a zoo in there,' the exhausted teacher will say as she crawls out of the room, hair in disarray and the scars of battle on her face.